Democracy and the American Revolution

Democracy and the American Revolution

Edited by Yuval Levin,
Adam J. White, and John Yoo

AEI Press

Publisher for the American Enterprise Institute
WASHINGTON, DC

Library of Congress Cataloging-in-Publication Data

Names: Levin, Yuval, editor. | White, Adam J., editor. | Yoo, John, editor.

Title: Democracy and the American Revolution / edited by Yuval Levin, Adam White, and John Yoo.
Description: Washington, DC : AEI Press, publisher for the American Enterprise Institute, [2024] | Series: We hold these truths; vol 1 | Includes bibliographical references. |
Identifiers: LCCN 2024026357 (print) | LCCN 2024026358 (ebook) | ISBN 9780844750613 (paperback) | ISBN 9780844750606 (hardback) | ISBN 9780844750620 (epub)
Subjects: LCSH: United States. Declaration of Independence. | United States—Politics and government—1775-1783. | Democracy—United States—History—18th century. | Deliberative democracy—United States—History—18th century.
Classification: LCC E221 .D456 2024 (print) | LCC E221 (ebook) | DDC 973.313—dc23/eng/20240702
LC record available at https://lccn.loc.gov/2024026357
LC ebook record available at https://lccn.loc.gov/2024026358

Publisher for the American Enterprise Institute
for Public Policy Research
1789 Massachusetts Avenue, NW
Washington, DC 20036
www.aei.org

Printed in the United States of America

Contents

Introduction

YUVAL LEVIN

July 4, 2026, will mark the 250th anniversary of the Declaration of Independence and, therefore, of the United States of America. That we can point to such a distinct starting point marks us as a modern nation, perhaps the first modern nation: No countries older than the United States, but almost all countries younger, can claim to know in this way exactly when they were born.

The Declaration itself insists it does not mark the beginning of the American people as a distinct society, but only one of those moments when

> it becomes necessary for one people to dissolve the political
> bands which have connected them with another, and to assume
> among the powers of the earth, the separate and equal station
> to which the Laws of Nature and of Nature's God entitle them.

But this was a strategic understatement, to put it mildly. There had never really been any such moment before, and there is no prior example of a people declaring to the world its reasons for becoming a newly independent nation. The American Revolution was essentially the first successful colonial revolt in the known history of humanity. And the colonists chose to announce their rebellion by declaring a set of universal truths about humanity and then rooting their new nation in those bold assertions. It was an even bigger moment than the Declaration claimed.

That we can mark the anniversary of such a moment offers us an opportunity for gratitude and celebration. The authors of the Declaration of Independence, and the people whom they led and represented, would surely have been surprised that their achievement has lasted for two and a half centuries—and that the nation they launched has become the most prosperous and dynamic society in history. We should be thankful to be the beneficiaries of their sacrifices and to have the chance to build on what they left us.

But to do that well, we should also treat this anniversary as an opportunity for reflection and thought. We should consider just what it was that began 250 years ago—what the American Revolution involved and achieved, what the nation it created meant at its origin, what it has come to mean since, and what it may mean in the future. This book, and the series of which it is a part, aims to reflect on precisely those questions.

That may sound like a strangely intellectual way to celebrate a birthday, but it is actually a distinctly and familiarly American form of patriotism. This country has always offered its people fodder for serious thought, and Americans have always looked on our country as both the home we love because it is ours and a kind of sociopolitical achievement that must be measured against its ideals. That our nation's 250th birthday will be a time for asking whether we are living up to those ideals is only natural.

But this book is also a distinctly intellectual form of celebration because it is the work of a community of scholars. The American Enterprise Institute is a venue for reflection—both theoretical and practical—on how the United States could best live up to its promise and how its people could be more happy, virtuous, free, and safe. We know that the nation's semiquincentennial will be marked by different individuals and groups in different ways, but in thinking about what our particular contribution might be, it seemed perfectly obvious that it would need to be an enduring intellectual product.

This has been the impetus behind AEI's "We Hold These Truths: America at 250" initiative. Over several years leading up to the anniversary, we are inviting scholars both within AEI and from other institutions to take up a series of themes important to understanding the American Revolution. These scholars represent various fields and viewpoints, so they will approach each of these themes from various angles that could allow their work in combination to offer a broad field of vision on the questions they address. The papers they produce will be published in a series of edited volumes intended to help Americans think more deeply and clearly about our nation's origins, character, and prospects.

Democracy and the American Revolution is the first of those books. Its chapters began as papers presented at an AEI conference held in Washington, DC, on November 15, 2023. Further volumes will consider the American Revolution in relation to other themes, such as religion, natural rights, the legacy of slavery, and the Constitution.

Democracy is our first theme because its connection to the American founding, while essential, is more complicated than it might first seem. The American revolutionaries launched their rebellion against Britain at least in some part as the result of what they took to be a democratic deficit: They objected to being taxed without being represented in Parliament. But the Declaration of Independence does not present itself as founding a democracy. Rather, it asserts indifference to particular forms of government, insisting that a people finding themselves misgoverned have the right "to institute new Government, laying its foundation on such principles and organizing its powers in such form, as to them shall seem most likely to effect their Safety and Happiness."

But here, too, the Declaration seems to engage in a kind of calculated understatement. The insistence that a legitimate government must secure the rights of its people and facilitate their safety and happiness places rather strict constraints on the range of forms it could plausibly take. And the particular complaints lodged against the British king sketch out by implication some of the boundaries of that range. We are told, for instance, that the king "has dissolved Representative Houses repeatedly, for opposing with manly firmness his invasions on the rights of the people," and that he "has refused for a long time, after such dissolutions, to cause others to be elected; whereby the Legislative powers, incapable of Annihilation, have returned to the People at large for their exercise." If these are reasons to rebel against the king, they certainly suggest a broadly democratic conception of the character of political legitimacy.

If we take democracy, as we should, to describe more than a formal system of government, it emerges that much more prominently in the drama of the American Revolution. If it is, as Alexis de Tocqueville suggested, more of a "social state," then surely we would have to say that the spirit of democracy was prominent among both the causes and effects of the American Revolution—indeed that, in a sense, it is what that revolution unleashed upon the world. Democracy is, in that respect, the natural first theme to take up in considering our founding's legacy.

In the chapters that follow, five eminent scholars of history and political thought explore how we ought to understand democracy and its connection to the American Revolution.

Gordon S. Wood considers the varied meanings of democracy and the range of ways they shaped the actions, ideas, and self-understandings of the American people in the era of the Revolution. He suggests that we should think about that era not as a single moment but as a period of gradual development in which a set of democratic concepts and a set of American practices and institutions shaped each other.

Bryan Garsten then explores the nature of the revolutionary spirit itself—that spark of independence that moved the founding generation to act boldly and has reappeared at key moments in our history. He argues that understanding that spirit as a kind of episodic passion is crucial to grasping the deepest meaning of the Declaration of Independence for our time.

Peter Berkowitz considers some of the ways we have misunderstood the Declaration, and he proposes to correct those by drawing on a set of both classical and modern political ideas. These, he believes, can help us better comprehend the nature of modern liberal democracy and the central place of the American founding in defining it.

Danielle Allen digs further into the Declaration itself and illuminates John Adams's underappreciated role as its coauthor, alongside Thomas Jefferson. She argues that, by better appreciating the part that Adams played in conceiving and articulating some of the Declaration's key concepts, especially the idea of the pursuit of happiness, we could more fully understand the ways that document sowed the seeds of the democratic age we inhabit.

And finally, Greg Weiner argues that the Declaration of Independence should be understood as a thoroughly democratic document. Drawing on Abraham Lincoln, he writes that the Declaration is an argument intended to persuade a majority to act together in defense of the fundamental rights of all human beings. It is therefore rooted in a conception of politics oriented to both pursuing the common good of society and securing the core natural rights of individuals, and it suggests that the two need not be contradictory.

The breadth of the arguments advanced in these chapters offers a sense of how broad the meaning of democracy might be. And their depth can help us see how profound an event the American founding was—and how important are the continuing stakes of the American experiment.

On this momentous anniversary, we are compelled to ask ourselves what kind of nation was brought into the world 250 years ago. "A democratic nation" certainly offers a strong opening attempt at an answer. Like this book, that answer must be understood as only one crucial part of a larger whole—but one that comes first with good reason.

1

A New Kind of Democracy

GORDON S. WOOD

Democracy has many meanings. For some, it may merely suggest a
government in which all adults can vote. For others, it may mean
simply majority rule, or it may denote a system of government that
protects minorities of all sorts—the assumption being that majorities
can take care of themselves. For still others, democracy may signify the
protection of individual rights and liberties—and signify that, without
these protections, voting and participation in government are meaningless. Finally, for many Americans, democracy may mean much more
than all these political mechanisms and principles, all the voting and
all the rights. It may transcend systems of government and become a
shorthand term that encompasses everything valuable about society
and culture: its freedom, its equality, and its respect for common, ordinary people.

All of these meanings of democracy have relevance today, and the
American Revolution created or enhanced all of them. In not much more
than a decade or two following the Declaration of Independence, America experienced the birth of modern democracy in its various expressions
and meanings. The Revolution created democracy as we understand it
today, as an all-powerful faith, a set of sacred principles and beliefs that
define and embrace not just our various governments but our entire society and culture as well.

From Subjects to Citizens

America today may be all about democracy, but that was not true at the time of the Declaration of Independence. Creating democracy was never the Revolution's goal; protecting liberty was. In 1776, the revolutionaries scarcely ever mentioned the terms "democracy" or "democratic." When they did use the word "democracy," they, like the ancient Greeks, often used it disparagingly. Sometimes they used it to denote the lowest order of society, and at other times they associated it with mobs and the civil disorder that preceded a dictator's takeover. At best they meant by it only a technical term of political science—a government ruled literally by the people at-large.

Many enlightened Americans agreed that ideally the people ought to govern themselves directly, but they realized that democracy in this literal sense was achieved only in the Greek city-states and New England town meetings. Actual self-government or simple democracy was not feasible for any large community. As one American polemicist stated in 1776, even the great 17th-century English radical Whig Algernon Sidney had written that he had known of "no such thing" as, "in the strict sense, (that is, pure Democracy,) where the People in themselves, and by themselves, perform all that belongs to Government," and if any such democracy had ever existed in the world, he had "nothing to say for it."[1]

America did not become a democracy in 1776 but a republic, or more accurately, 13 independent republics. Beyond repudiating hereditary rule, republicanism did not prescribe a particular form of government. It was more of a spirit, a set of ideals and values for shaping society and culture. It challenged the primary assumptions and practices of monarchy—its hierarchy, its inequality, its devotion to kinship, its patriarchy, and its patronage. It offered new conceptions of the individual, the family, the state, and the individual's relationship to the family, the state, and other individuals.

Becoming republics in 1776 marked a change of society, not just of government. People were to be "changed," wrote the South Carolina physician and historian David Ramsay, "from subjects to citizens," and "the difference is immense." He added:

> Subject is derived from the latin words, *sub* and *jacio*, and means one who is *under* the power of another; but a citizen is an *unit* of a mass of free people, who, collectively, possess sovereignty.

> Subjects look up to a master, but citizens are so far equal, that none have hereditary rights superior to others. Each citizen of a free state contains, within himself, by nature and the constitution, as much of the common sovereignty as another.[2]

The republican Revolution assumed the rulers derived all their authority from the people. But deriving authority did not mean the people actually ruled themselves. Instead, the people, as Alexander Hamilton wrote, had a right "to a *share* in the government."[3] Indeed, that share was essential to the protection of liberty, which was a key purpose of government. But in a large modern state, how was that presence, or that share, in government to be realized? The impossibility of convening the whole people of the society, it was thought, had led to the great English discovery of representation—"substituting the few in the room of the many," as some Americans described it.

The British people's representation in the House of Commons and the colonists' representation in their 13 provincial legislatures constituted "the democratical parts" of their constitutions.[4] But for the working of a proper constitution and the protection of liberty, champions of this approach believed this democracy had to be mixed or balanced with monarchy and aristocracy. Indeed, 18th-century English speakers used the term "democracy" favorably and almost always with "monarchy" and "aristocracy"—as an essential part of the mixed or balanced constitution of Great Britain and the "little models of the English constitution" in the provincial governments of North America.[5]

The theory of mixed or balanced government was as old as the ancient Greeks and had dominated Western political thinking for centuries. It was based on the classical categorization of forms of government into three ideal types: monarchy, aristocracy, and democracy. That scheme was derived from the number and character of the ruling power: the one, the few, and the many.

Each of these simple forms possessed a certain quality of excellence. For monarchy, it was order or energy; for aristocracy, it was wisdom; and for democracy, it was honesty or goodness. Maintaining these peculiar qualities, however, depended on the forms of government standing fast on an imagined spectrum of power. Yet experience had tragically taught that none of these simple forms by itself could remain stable. Left alone, each ran headlong into perversion in the eager search by the rulers (whether one, few, or many) for more power.

Monarchy lunged toward its extremity and ended in despotism. Aristocracy, located midway on the band of power, pulled in both directions and created faction and division. And democracy, seeking more power in the hands of the people, degenerated into anarchy and tumult.

The mixed or balanced polity was designed to prevent these perversions. By including all the classic simple forms of government in the same constitution, the forces pulling in one direction would be counterbalanced by other forces, and stability would result. Only through this reciprocal sharing of political power by the one, the few, and the many could the desirable qualities of each be preserved. As John Adams declared in 1772, "Liberty depends upon an exact Ballance, a nice Counterpoise of all the Powers of the state. . . . The best Governments of the World have been mixed."[6]

Although Americans in 1776 were throwing off monarchy and establishing republics, most of them had no intention of abandoning this celebrated theory of mixed or balanced government. They still believed their new republican state governments ought to embody the classic principles of monarchy, aristocracy, and democracy. Consequently, in nearly all of their new state constitutions drafted in 1776 and 1777, the revolutionaries created republican versions of a balanced constitution—with single though considerably weakened governors to express the one, with upper houses or senates to express the few, and with powerful and greatly enlarged houses of representatives to express the many. In fact, so much power was granted to the popular houses of representation in the revolutionary constitutions of 1776 that some Americans, like Richard Henry Lee of Virginia, concluded that their new governments were "very much of the democratic kind," even though "a Governor and second branch of legislation are admitted."[7]

In several states, particularly in Pennsylvania, some revolutionaries deliberately rejected incorporating the theory of balanced government in their new state constitutions. Radical forces in Pennsylvania in 1776 argued that a mixed government that included a governor and senate implied the existence of monarchical and aristocratic elements in their society that the republican revolution supposedly had abolished. "There is but one rank of men in America," the Pennsylvania radicals argued, "and therefore, . . . there should be only one representation of them in a government."[8] The creation of a senate, they warned, would lead to the rise of a house of lords and an aristocracy. Consequently, the constitution makers in Pennsylvania, in emulation of what they believed was "the Ancient Saxon constitution," erected a simple government composed of a single legislative body with no governor and no senate or upper house. It was as close to an 18th-century version of democracy as seemed feasible for a large community. But because this democracy was not balanced or mixed with monarchical and aristocratic elements, many considered the Pennsylvania Constitution a monster that should be replaced as soon as possible.

In 1776, therefore, democracy was still essentially a technical term of political theory—referring to government literally by the people, which was an impossibility for huge numbers of people. But from the beginning of the revolutionary movement, Americans sought to overcome this impossibility in every conceivable way, and in the process they became the first society in the modern world to bring ordinary people into the affairs of government—not just as voters but as actual rulers. This participation of common people in government became the essence of American democracy, and the Revolution made it so.

Actual Representation

The issue of democracy in the Revolution began with the imperial debate leading up to the break with Great Britain. In 1765, Parliament enacted the Stamp Act, a direct tax on various paper items in the colonies. The colonists responded passionately, arguing that, since they had not elected any members to the House of Commons, they were not represented in Parliament, which meant they were being taxed without their consent. The British responded by arguing that the colonists were virtually represented in Parliament and thus had consented to the tax. The British claimed that people were represented in Parliament not by the process of election—which the British considered to be incidental to representation—but by the mutuality of interests that members of Parliament were presumed to share with all Britons, including those, like the colonists, who did not actually vote for them. After all, the British argued, cities in England like Manchester and Birmingham with 50,000 or more inhabitants elected no members to Parliament but were, nonetheless, considered to be virtually represented in the House of Commons.

To most Americans, this argument was incomprehensible. They believed in what they called actual representation. If the people were to be properly represented in a legislature, not only did they have to actually vote for the members of the legislature, but they also had to be represented by members whose numbers were more or less proportionate to the size of the population they spoke for. For Americans, election was not incidental to representation, as it was for the British, but its criterion, and this required the closest possible connections between the representatives and their constituents.

This difference of opinion was rooted in what was already a distinctly American evolution of the British political model. The colonists were used to voting for the representatives in their provincial legislatures. Two-thirds of adult white males had the right to vote, although turnout was usually very low unless some important issue like religion was at stake. Since in Britain only one in six adult males could vote, the American electorate was proportionately the largest in the world. And nowhere outside the English-speaking world in the 18th century did people vote for their leaders at all.

Of course, by today's standards, that democracy was severely limited. In the colonies, all women and any men without sufficient property did not possess the suffrage, which was true in England as well. Since all women and males who lacked a 40-shilling freehold were considered dependent on others, they were deemed to have no wills of their own and thus could be easily manipulated by those with power and property. This was the rationale for excluding them from the suffrage. Although many American males worked tirelessly over the several decades following independence to eliminate all property qualifications for voting and create universal white male suffrage, very few as yet envisioned women participating in politics. For a brief period between 1790 and 1807, unmarried, property-holding women took advantage of a quirk in the New Jersey Constitution and exercised the franchise. But when the loophole was closed in 1807 and New Jersey women stopped voting, no one seemed to much care.

But the most excruciating failure to live up to democratic theory (and basic justice and decency) was the presence of black slavery. Of the total American population of two and a half million in 1776, one-fifth—consisting of 500,000 men, women, and children of African descent—were enslaved. The revolutionary leaders realized immediately that their revolution on behalf of liberty was totally inconsistent with the holding of slaves and with all forms of unfreedom.

Consequently, upon America's independence, the majority of the states began moving against slavery, initiating what became the first great anti-slavery movement in world history. Although nearly 90 percent of slaves lived in the South, northerners possessed nearly 50,000 slaves, a not insignificant number. By 1804, all the northern states had legally abolished slavery and had brought an end to bonded servitude. But despite some faltering efforts at abolition in Virginia—which had the most slaves of any state, with 200,000, or 40 percent of its population—the southern states refused to follow the North's lead and abolish the institution. This failure initiated the sectional division that would eventually lead to the Civil War.

Thus the American democracy that emerged from the Revolution remained essentially a northern phenomenon, for, as James Madison later admitted, "In proportion as slavery prevails in a State, the Government, however democratic in name, must be aristocratic in fact."[9] The slave-holding southern states never fully experienced the kind of democracy that came to characterize the northern states, even if they experienced elements of the distinctly novel democratic culture that began to emerge on this continent.

Egalitarian Dynamism

The Revolution turned out to be much more radical than many of its leaders expected. It released the aspirations and interests of tens of thousands of middling people—commercial farmers, petty merchants, small-time traders, and artisans of various sorts—all eager to buy and sell and get rich, creating a wild, scrambling, bustling, individualistic democratic world unlike anything that had ever existed before.

The eight years of war brought into being hosts of new manufacturing and entrepreneurial interests and made market farmers out of husband-men who had rarely ever traded out of their neighborhoods. The revolutionary governments issued hundreds of millions of dollars in paper money, which blanketed the continent. By 1778, said South Carolina merchant-planter Henry Laurens, president of the Continental Congress, "the demand for money" was no longer "confined to the capital towns and cities within a small circle of trading merchants, but spread over a surface of 1,600 miles in length and 300 [miles] broad."[10] The war seemed to have created a society in which, as one commissary agent complained, "Every Man buys in order to sell again."[11]

Of course, many people went into debt. But debt in this emerging capitalist society was not a sign of poverty; it was a sign of ambitious aspirations. Issuing paper money was not intended simply to relieve debt. It was capital, and it was necessary for buying land or livestock, setting up a shop, or fulfilling other dreams. The inflation caused by printing paper money hurt creditors and those on fixed incomes, but those who were most active in all the buying and selling and the movement of goods could and did prosper from such inflation.

By the end of the war in the early 1780s, there was a great deal of economic dislocation and confusion. But at the same time, much of the country was bursting with energy and enterprise, and people were on the move in search of opportunities. They were spilling over the mountains into the newly acquired western territories with astonishing rapidity and clashing with and ultimately overwhelming the native peoples in the process. Despite a slackening of immigration and the loss of tens of thousands of British loyalists, the 1780s experienced the fastest rate of population growth in any decade of American history—in no small part because young people, optimistic about future prosperity, were marrying earlier and thus having more children. "There is not upon the face of the earth a body of people more happy or rising into consequence with more rapid stride, than the Inhabitants of the United States of America," Charles Thomson, secretary of the Continental Congress, told Thomas Jefferson, minister to France, in 1786. "Population is increasing, new houses building, new lands clearing, new settlements forming and new manufactures establishing with a rapidity beyond conception."[12]

Nothing contributed more to this explosion of energy than the idea of equality. Equality was in fact the most radical and most powerful ideological force let loose by the Revolution. Its appeal was far more potent than the revolutionaries anticipated. Once invoked, the idea of equality could not be contained, and it tore through American society and culture with awesome power.

Equality lay at the heart of republican citizenship; it was, Ramsay wrote, "the life and soul of commonwealth."[13] By equality the revolutionaries meant most obviously equality of opportunity, inciting genius to action and opening up careers to men of talent and virtue while destroying kinship and patronage as sources of authority. With social movement both up and down founded on individual ability and character, however, it was assumed that no distinctions would have time to harden or be perpetuated across generations. Thus, equality of opportunity would help encourage a rough equality of condition.

Since antiquity, many theorists had assumed that republicanism required a rough equality of property holding among its citizens. Although most Americans in 1776 accepted different degrees of property holding, they also took for granted that a society could not long remain republican if only a tiny minority controlled most of the wealth and the bulk of the population remained dependent servants or landless laborers.

Equality was related to independence; Jefferson's original draft of the Declaration of Independence stated that "all men are created free & independent." Men were equal in that no one of them should be dependent on the will of another, and property made this independence possible. Americans in 1776 therefore concluded that they were naturally fit for republicanism precisely because they were "a people of property; almost every man is a freeholder."[14]

Yet in the end, equality came to mean even more than this to Americans. If equality had meant only equality of opportunity or a rough equality of property holding, it could never have become, as it has, the single most powerful and radical ideological force in all of American history. Equality became so potent for Americans because it came to mean that everyone was really the same as everyone else—not just at birth, not just in talent or property or wealth, and not just in some transcendental religious sense of the equality of all souls. Ordinary Americans came to believe that no one, in a basic down-to-earth and day-in-and-day-out manner, was really better than anyone else.

When the wealthy former governor of South Carolina, John Rutledge, sought in 1784 to have the state legislature banish William Thompson, a tavern keeper, from the state for an alleged personal insult (having denied Rutledge's slave access to his tavern's roof to watch fireworks), Thompson took his defense to the press on behalf, he wrote, of the people or "those more especially, who go at this day, under the opprobrious appellation of, the *Lower Orders of Men*." The tavern keeper recounted how he, "a *wretch* of no higher rank in the Commonwealth than that of Common-Citizen," had been debased by "those *self-exalted* characters, who affect to compose the *grand hierarchy* of the State, . . . for having dared to dispute with a *John Rutledge*, or any of that NABOB *tribe*." Undoubtedly, Thompson wrote, Rutledge had "conceived me his inferior." But Thompson, like many other middling men in these years, could no longer "comprehend the *inferiority*."[5]

Middling men like Thompson were challenging their presumed superiors everywhere. Some of them were even engaging in politics, which resulted in men of more humble and rural origins and less education than had hitherto sat in the colonial assemblies gaining election to the greatly enlarged state legislatures. Some of the new houses of representatives were two and three times as big as than their colonial predecessors. In New Hampshire, for example, the colonial house of representatives in 1765 had contained only 34 members, almost all well-to-do gentlemen from the coastal region around Portsmouth. By 1786 the state's House of Representatives numbered 88 members, most of whom were ordinary farmers or men of moderate wealth from the state's western areas. Not only did these representatives have a hard time passing as gentlemen, but they were eager to promote the interests of their occupations.

In all the states, electioneering and the open competition for office increased dramatically, aided by somewhat enlarged electorates. The high levels of incumbency and stability that had characterized the colonial assemblies on the eve of the Revolution were now reversed, and the annual elections for the legislatures (an innovation outside of New England) often saw half or more of the representatives in the states turned over in any one year.

Under these turbulent circumstances, the state legislatures could scarcely fulfill what many revolutionaries in 1776 had assumed was their republican responsibility—to promote a unitary public interest distinguishable from the many private and parochial interests of people. By the 1780s it was obvious to many that "a spirit of *locality*" was destroying "the aggregate interests of the Community."[16] Everywhere the gentry complained of popular legislative practices that we today take for granted—parochialism, horse trading, and pork barreling that benefited special interest groups. Each representative, grumbled Ezra Stiles, president of Yale College, was concerned only with the particular interests of his electors. Whenever a bill was read in the legislature, "every one instantly thinks how it will affect his constituents."[17] Instead of electing men to office "for their abilities, integrity and patriotism," the people were much more likely to vote for someone "from some mean, interested, or capricious motive." They

> choose a man, because he will vote for a new town, or a new county, or in favor of a memorial; because he is noisy in blaming those who are in office, has confidence enough to suppose that he could do better, and impudence enough to tell the people so; or because he possesses, in a supereminent degree, the all-prevailing popular talent of coaxing and flattering.[18]

Critics summed up all this behavior as the "excess of democracy."[19]

By the 1780s the press was full of warnings that "our situation is critical and dangerous" and that "our vices" were plunging us into "national ruin."[20] America, they said, was in crisis. And the cause was too much democracy in the states; the lower houses were running amok with erratic legislation.

Reformers proposed all sorts of solutions. Some wanted stronger executives and stronger senates to offset the power of the lower houses. Others began to look to state judges as a means of restraining the rampaging popular legislatures. By 1786, William Plumer, a future US senator and governor of New Hampshire, concluded that the very "existence" of America's elective governments had come to depend on the judiciary. Because of the judiciary's ability to measure laws against the state constitutions, it "is the only body of men who will have an effective check upon a numerous Assembly."[21] But in the 1780s no one could foresee how powerful judges would become, and most elites looked to a new national constitution as the best remedy for the excessive democracy in the states.

Mutability and Injustice

Many delegates to the Constitutional Convention who met in Philadelphia in 1787 were ready to accept Madison's Virginia Plan with its proposed national congressional veto over all state laws precisely because they shared his disgust with what was going on in the state legislatures. "The vile State governments are sources of pollution, which will contaminate the American name for ages. . . . Smite them," Henry Knox urged Rufus King, who was sitting in the Philadelphia Convention. "Smite them in the name of God and the people."[22]

The lack of "*wisdom* and steadiness" in lawmaking, wrote Madison in 1785, was "the grievance complained of in all our republics."[23] In summing up America's crisis in a 1787 memorandum titled "Vices of the Political System of the United States," Madison focused almost entirely on the erratic behavior of the state legislatures—on the "multiplicity," "mutability," and "injustice" of the state laws.[24] There were more laws, he said, passed by the state assemblies in the decade since independence than had been passed in the entire colonial period. And those laws had been constantly changing to the point where judges scarcely knew what the law was. But most alarming, said Madison, was the injustice of much of this state legislation.

Especially upsetting to Madison and other prominent gentry was the proliferation of paper money emissions, together with the stay laws and other debtor-relief legislation that hurt the minority of creditors and violated individual property rights. Entrepreneurial-minded debtors in the states were using their majorities in the legislatures to abuse the minorities of creditors who had lent them money, which the debtors used to promote their commercial interests. To gentry creditors up and down the continent, these emissions of paper money that led to inflation and the depreciation of the currency seemed to be a great injustice that struck at the heart of the social order. "The Cry for Paper Money," exclaimed Adams in 1786, "is downright Wickedness and Dishonesty. Every Man must see that it is the worst Engine of Knavery that ever was invented."[25]

Unlike the English aristocracy, who lived off the rents from long-term tenants, the American gentry elites, who constituted whatever aristocracy America possessed, had relatively few tenants, land being so much more widely available in the New World. The American gentry relied instead on the interest earned from money out on loan. By lending money to members of their local communities, they were in effect acting as bankers in a society that had few, if any, banking institutions. As creditors, they were especially vulnerable to inflation and the currency depreciation caused by excessive issues of paper money.

George Washington, who was a planter, banker, and commander in chief of the American revolutionary army, became furious with the way his debtors had used the depreciation of paper money to scam him while he was away fighting the British. These scoundrels, he complained in 1785, had "taken advantage of my absence and the tender laws, to discharge their debts with a shilling or a six pence to the pound." At the same time, he had "to pay in specie at the real value"[26] to those British merchants in London to whom he owed money. All this debtor-relief legislation convinced him the following year that virtue had "in a great degree, taken its departure from our Land."[27]

The expressions of democracy in the state legislation of the 1780s were creating a new, unprecedented, and unanticipated kind of tyranny. Traditionally, excesses of democracy had led to anarchy, licentiousness, and the breakdown of law and order. But in America everything was different. When Tory loyalist Daniel Leonard raised the possibility that all the democracy expressed in the proliferating popular committees in 1775 might get out of hand and become despotic, Adams dismissed the idea without any hesitation. The notion that the people, who loved liberty, might tyrannize themselves was illogical. "A democratical despotism," he wrote, "is a contradiction in terms."[28]

But a decade later, Adams had changed his mind, as had many other American leaders. A massive rethinking of the assumptions of 1776 led to the Constitutional Convention in 1787 and plans for reforming the national government, which, it was hoped, would, among other things, deal with the "excess of democracy" that had emerged in the states. With his Virginia Plan, Madison did not intend to move in a monarchical direction to cope with the vices of America's political system. Instead, he wanted "a republican remedy for the diseases most incident to republican government."[29] For him and for many others, the stakes were high. The convention meeting in Philadelphia in 1787 to frame a new constitution would "decide forever the fate of republican government."[30]

Madison and other leaders thought the source of the problem of rampaging and abusive majorities in the states lay mainly in the kinds of people who were elected to the state legislatures, especially the lower and more democratic houses. Too many narrow-minded and illiberal middle-class people—with their own interests to promote—had seized control of the state legislatures.

It was not just a lack of ability that rendered middle-class artisans, farmers, and tradesmen unsuited to important governmental office in the eyes of the American gentry. It was their deep involvement in work, trade, and business—their occupations, their very interestedness—that made such ignoble men unsuitable for high office. They lacked the requisite liberal, disinterested, cosmopolitan outlook that presumably was possessed only by enlightened and educated persons—only by gentlemen.

Earlier efforts in the 1760s and 1770s by carpenters, butchers, shoemakers, and those with other artisanal "interests" to promote their participation in revolutionary politics had been easily dismissed by the dominant patriot elite. It was inconceivable to someone like William Henry Drayton of South Carolina that gentlemen with a liberal education (in his case, at Oxford) should have to consult on the difficulties of government

> with men who never were in a way to study, or to advise upon any points, but rules how to cut up a beast in the market to the best advantage, to cobble an old shoe in the neatest manner, or to build a necessary house.[31]

Drayton was willing to admit that "the profanum vulgus" was "a species of mankind" and even that such artisans were "a useful and necessary part of society." But, he said, those sorts of men were not meant to govern. "Nature never intended that such men should be profound politicians or able statesmen."[32]

Drayton was speaking out of a classical tradition of virtuous political leadership that went back to Aristotle. It was assumed that only autonomous individuals, free of interested ties and paid by no masters, were capable of virtue or disinterestedness—the term the revolutionary leaders most often used as a synonym for classical virtue. It meant impartiality and fairness.

Many 18th-century British thinkers, ranging from Adam Smith to the radical Whigs John Trenchard and Thomas Gordon—whose writings as "Cato" were especially popular in the colonies—had concluded that the increasingly commercialized character of modern society made classical disinterestedness increasingly rare. Only "a very small part of mankind," wrote "Cato," "have capacities large enough to judge of the whole of things."[33] Traditional classical thinking assumed that the growing numbers of ordinary middling people were so caught up in their workaday occupations and interests that they were incapable of making disinterested judgments about the society—incapable, in other words, of being political leaders. Even wealthy merchants were too self-interested to be leaders. Only "those few," wrote Smith in *Wealth of Nations*, "attached to no particular occupation themselves, have leisure and inclination to examine the occupations of other people."[34] For Smith the ideal leaders of government were the English landed aristocracy, members of which were free of the marketplace and thus capable of disinterested judgments. The "revenue" the landed gentry received from the rents of their estates, said Smith, was unique. It "costs them neither labour nor care, but comes to them, as it were, of its own accord, and independent of any plan or project of their own."[35]

In America the southern planter gentry, including founders such as Jefferson and Madison, whose leisure was facilitated by the labor of their African slaves, believed they came closest to realizing the classical image of disinterested leadership, and they made the most of it throughout their history. In northern American society, independent and leisured gentry standing above the interests of the marketplace were harder to find, but the ideal remained strong. In 1767 the wealthy Philadelphia lawyer John Dickinson posed as a Pennsylvania farmer in writing his pamphlet in defense of America. He wanted to assure his readers that he was a simple disinterested farmer, "contented" and "undisturbed by worldly hopes or fears."[36]

Rich merchants in international trade brought wealth into the society, but any claims of disinterestedness they might make were tainted by their concern for personal profit. Perhaps only a classical education that made "ancient manners familiar," as Richard Jackson told his friend Benjamin Franklin, could "produce a reconciliation between disinterestedness and commerce; a thing we often see, but almost always in men of a liberal education."[37] Artisans who worked with their hands, of course, could never be impartial and disinterested leaders, which is why Franklin had retired from his printing business at age 42 to engage in politics.

By the 1780s the revolutionary leaders were expressing ever-mounting doubts about the American people's capacity for virtue. Because the society had become so flush with paper money, buying and selling, and the proliferation of interests, gentlemen up and down the continent realized that too many parochial and interested men had become representatives in the state legislatures. Too many middling sorts such as Abraham Clark, a surveyor and self-educated lawyer from New Jersey, and Abraham Yates Jr., a onetime shoemaker and wine merchant from Albany,

New York, had pandered "to the vulgar and sordid notions of the populace" and exploited the republican emphasis on equality to vault into positions in government that they were ill-equipped to hold.[38]

Although these middling sorts were often shrewd and very smart, they had not gone to college and thus had not received a classical education that would presumably have tempered their selfish and acquisitive instincts, or so the gentry thought. To many of the liberally educated gentry, this meant that such middling legislators were not really gentlemen and were thus unqualified to be political leaders. The source of the 1780s crisis, said Robert R. Livingston, chancellor of New York and a member of one of the state's great aristocratic families, was the way in which the state legislatures had been taken over by men "unimproved by education and unrefined by honor."[39]

One of the smartest of those middling characters was William Findley, an ex-weaver and a Scotch-Irish immigrant who became the prime object of Hugh Henry Brackenridge's satiric comic novel, *Modern Chivalry*, the "great moral" of which was the "evil of men seeking office for which they are not qualified."[40] In the Pennsylvania legislature Findley became a keen supporter of the paper-money interests of his constituents in the Pittsburgh area, and he was precisely the kind of narrow-minded and illiberal middling legislator that elites like Madison disliked and feared.

In a debate in the Pennsylvanian assembly in 1786 over the rechartering of the Bank of North America, Findley accused the bank's legislative supporters, including the wealthy merchant and Revolution financier Robert Morris, of having a selfish interest in the bank. But instead of simply pointing out that the bank's supporters had no right "to be a judge in their own cause," Findley, who refused to be intimidated by any of his so-called superiors, accepted the investors' interest in the bank and found nothing improper in their efforts to obtain its rechartering.[41] As the bank's directors and shareholders, Findley said, they could hardly be expected to do otherwise; "any others in their situation . . . would do as they did." Findley went on to contend that Morris and the other bank investors had every "right to advocate their own cause, on the floor of this house." But they had no right to protest when others realize "that it is their own cause they are advocating; and to give credit to their opinions, and to think of their votes accordingly."[42] In one of the most remarkable anticipations of modern democratic politics made during the revolutionary era, Findley said such open promotion of private selfish interests by legislators was quite legitimate as long as it was open and aboveboard and not disguised by specious claims of genteel disinterestedness.

If the representatives were elected to promote the particular interests and private causes of their constituents, then the idea that such representatives should be disinterested gentlemen—squire worthies called by duty to shoulder the burdens of public service—had become archaic. In this new bustling America of many interests where the candidate for the legislature "has a cause of his own to advocate," said Findley, "interest will dictate the propriety of canvassing for a seat."[43] In other words, it was now legitimate for politically ambitious middling men, with interests and causes to promote, to run and compete for electoral office.

With these remarks in 1786, Findley was anticipating all the modern democratic political developments of the immediately succeeding decades in America: the increased electioneering and competitive politics, the open promotion of private interests in legislation, the acceptance of the legitimacy of political parties, the extension of the actual and direct representation of particular groups in government, and the eventual weakening, if not the repudiation, of the classical republican ideal that legislators were supposed to be disinterested promoters of a public good that was separate from the private-marketplace interests of the society.

Madison knew only too well the kinds of men and the kinds of middling interests Findley represented. In his famous *Federalist* 10, he set forth his profound objections to the democratic politics that he saw emerging in the American states since the Declaration of Independence. No man is allowed to be a judge in his own cause, wrote Madison,

> because his interest would certainly bias his judgment, and, not improbably, corrupt his integrity. With equal, nay with

greater reason, a body of men are unfit to be both judges and parties at the same time; yet what are many of the most important acts of legislation, but so many judicial determinations, not indeed concerning the rights of single persons, but concerning the rights of large bodies of citizens? And what are the different classes of legislators but advocates and parties to the causes which they determine? Is a law proposed concerning private debts? It is a question to which the creditors are parties on one side and the debtors on the other. Justice ought to hold the balance between them. Yet the parties are, and must be, themselves the judges; and the most numerous party, or in other words, the most powerful faction must be expected to prevail.[44]

Since the popular colonial assemblies had often begun as courts (like the General Court of Massachusetts) and much of their legislation had resembled adjudication, Madison's use of judicial imagery to describe the factional and interest-group politics in the state legislatures was not misplaced. But this judicial imagery did prevent Madison from thinking freshly in solving the problem of modern democratic legislative politics that he had so brilliantly diagnosed. He still hoped in a traditional fashion that the new federal government might become, as he put it, a "disinterested & dispassionate umpire in disputes between different passions & interests in the State."[45]

Constitutional Democracy

The federal Constitution of 1787 was, in part at least, intended to be a solution to the problems of interest-group politics plaguing the state legislatures. Yet how was such a strong national government supposed to avoid the majoritarian factionalism in the states? One of the Constitution's leading opponents, James Winthrop, scion of the great Winthrop family of Massachusetts, saw at once the problem. "The complaints against the separate [state] governments, even by the friends of the new plan," wrote Winthrop in his "Agrippa" essays, "are not that they have not power enough, but that they are disposed to make a bad use of what power they have." Surely, he wrote, the Constitution's supporters were reasoning badly "when they purpose to set up a government possess'd of much more extensive powers . . . and subject to much smaller checks" than the existing state governments possessed and were subject to.[46] How would the new national government avoid the majoritarian factionalism afflicting the states?

Madison for one was quite aware of the pointedness of this objection. "It may be asked," he wrote in a letter to his friend Jefferson, in October 1787, "how private rights will be more secure under the Guardianship of the General Government than under the State Governments, since they are both founded on the republican principle which refers the ultimate decision to the will of the majority."[47] What, in other words, was different about the new federal government that would keep its majorities from passing the same kinds of oppressive legislation that the state governments had passed?

Madison's answer, which was the key to his Virginia Plan, had two parts. First, in the new federal government, the arena of politics would be expanded to encompass the whole nation. In this enlarged republic, the clashing interests and factions would be so numerous that they would have difficulty in coming together to form factious majorities. They would tend to neutralize themselves and thus allow "men who possess the most attractive merit and the most diffusive and established characters" to gain office and promote the public good.[48]

Madison took his cue from what had happened with religion in America. It was the multiplicity of denominations in America and the inability of any one of them to dominate that led to them accepting the neutralization of the state in religious matters. This competition among numerous denominations had permitted secular-minded men such as him and Jefferson to shape public policy and, in Virginia, to separate the state from all religions in an unprecedented manner.

Second, Madison hoped that the great height of the new federal government would prevent the narrow-minded and illiberal middling sorts from vaulting into power. This would permit more cosmopolitan and enlightened men to hold office. Madison called this a process of "filtrations."[49] By enlarging the electorate and decreasing the number of representatives, the new federal structure would act like a sieve filtering "from the mass of the Society the purest and noblest characters which it contains."[50]

Although the House of Representatives in the new federal government was to represent the entire national population of four million people, it comprised only 65 members, smaller than most state legislatures. Madison and his fellow Federalists, the name by which the Constitution's supporters shrewdly chose to call themselves, hoped these fewer numbers were more likely to be better educated and more enlightened than the hundreds who sat in each of the state legislatures. The five congressmen from North Carolina in the new national government, for example, were apt to be more respectable and enlightened, more likely to be college graduates, and more likely to be gentlemen than the 232 who sat in the North Carolina legislature.

In the ratification debates over the Constitution, its opponents (who came to be called Anti-Federalists) saw at once what the Constitution's supporters were up to, and they claimed loudly and continually that the Federalists were trying to foist an aristocracy on America.

It went almost without saying, they insisted, that the awesome president and the exalted Senate, "a compound of *monarchy* and *aristocracy*,"[51] would be dangerously far removed from the people. But even the House of Representatives, which "should be a true picture of the people,"[52] was without "a tincture of democracy." The "democratic branch"[53] of the government, the House of Representatives, which presumably should possess "the same interests, feelings, opinions, and views the people themselves would were they all assembled,"[54] was, with its scant 65 members, "a mere shred or rag"[55] of the people's power and hardly a match for the government's monarchical and aristocratic branches. "In fact," declared a Maryland opponent of the Constitution, "no order or class of the people will be represented in the House of Representatives called the Democratic Branch but the rich and wealthy."[56] The filtration process alone, they said, revealed that the proposed Constitution was nothing but an out-and-out aristocratic document.

In response, the Federalists expressed surprise. There was no aristocracy in America, they said. It was true: There was nothing in the new United States comparable to the hereditary nobilities of England and Europe. But, as the French minister to the United States, Louis Otto, noted, in America "there is a class of men denominated 'gentlemen,' who, by reason of their wealth, their talents, their education, their families, or the offices they hold, aspire to a preeminence which the people refuse to grant them."[57]

These so-called gentlemen, said the Anti-Federalists—in words that echoed those of Findley in 1786—had no right to rule simply because of their wealth, talents, and education; they were just one interest among all the other diverse interests of American society. That society, said the Anti-Federalists, comprised a mixture of "many different classes or orders of people, Merchants, Farmers, Planter Mechanics and Gentry or wealthy Men."[58] (In modern terms they might have added races and ethnicities to the diversity.) No one of them possessed any special disinterested character, and no one of them could be truly acquainted with the "*Situation and Wants*" of the others. Lawyers and planters had their own special interests and could never be "adequate judges of tradesmen's concerns."[59] Consequently, the only "fair representation" in government, declared the "Federal Farmer" (probably the self-educated petty merchant and lawyer Melancton Smith of New York, one of the most distinguished writers opposed to the Constitution), ought to be one in which "every order of men in the community . . . can have a share in it."[60] This extreme expression of actual representation was democracy as the Anti-Federalists, shaped by the theory and practice of American political life, understood it.

Confronted with these kinds of arguments—that every trade, every occupation, and every interest had a right to be represented in government by its own kind—most Federalists could only shake their heads in disbelief. It was impractical, said some Federalists, including Hamilton in *Federalist* 35. "The idea of an actual representation of all classes of the people, by persons of each class," he wrote, "is altogether visionary." Hamilton went on to argue that artisans could have their interests looked after by merchants and farmers by landlords and planters, but the best, most impartial representatives were members of the learned professions, by which he meant mainly lawyers. Unlike merchants, mechanics, and farmers, the liberally educated professions, he wrote, "truly form no distinct interest in society." They "will feel a neutrality to the rivalships between the different branches of industry" and thus will be most able to play the role of "an impartial arbiter" among society's diverse interests.[61]

Most Federalists realized this was not an altogether convincing refutation of the Anti-Federalist idea of representation, since lawyers themselves were seen as interested parties. Instead, most Federalists conceived of the people as a sovereign entity encompassing the whole society parceling out bits and pieces of its power to agents in all parts of every level of the United States government. Thus, ironically, in the process of contesting the Anti-Federalists, supporters of the Constitution ended up turning the national republic and all the separate state republics into democracies.

To counter the Anti-Federalists, the Constitution's proponents drew on another aspect of the idea of actual representation that the colonists had used in the 1760s to explain their opposition to the Stamp Act. Unlike the British idea of virtual representation, which made voting incidental to representation, the Americans' concept of actual representation made voting the criterion of representation: One had to vote for a delegate to be represented by him. The Federalists realized they could now use this idea of actual representation to justify the Constitution as a thoroughly democratic document. "The right of representing," said James Wilson in the ratification debates, "is conferred by the act of electing."[62]

Consequently, the Federalists claimed, all elected parts of the new federal government—the president, the Senate, and the House of Representatives—were the people's representative agents, and as such there was no reason for the people to fear them. Once grasped, this idea of representation was extended to involve all elected officials at the state and local levels. Governors, senators, and even judges—holders of any office that derived its authority from the people—were now considered to be representative of the people. To be sure, the members of the houses of representatives were the more "immediate representatives,"[63] but they were no longer the full and exclusive representatives of the people. The people were represented everywhere in America's governments. "The federal and State governments," wrote Madison in *Federalist* 46, "are in fact but different agents and trustees of the people, constituted with different powers, and designed for different purposes."[64] The American people, unlike people in Europe, were not an estate, an order, or a portion of the society; they were the source of all government.

Americans now told themselves that no people before them, not even the English, had ever understood the principle of representation as they had. The world "left to America the glory and happiness of forming a government where representation shall at once supply the basis and the cement of the superstructure," said Wilson (the most underappreciated founder) in 1788, "diffusing this vital principle throughout all the different divisions and departments of the government."[65] Representation, said Madison in *Federalist* 63, was "the pivot" on which the whole American system of government moved.[66]

Because their governments were so new and distinctive, Americans groped for terms adequate to describe them. And since the people were represented everywhere, in every part of every government, the governments had to be thoroughly democratic. Indeed, said John Stevens of New Jersey, election by the people, and not the strength of the lower houses in the legislatures, made "our governments the most democratic that ever have existed anywhere."[67]

By using popular and democratic rhetoric to justify the ratification of the Constitution, the Federalists tended to obscure their intentions, which set the stage for continual historical controversy over the nature of the Constitution—whether it was an aristocratic or democratic document. Clearly Madison and his fellow Federalists designed the

Constitution in part at least to channel and contain the democracy that was running wild in the states, but in the end, their remedy didn't work out quite as they had expected. The new federal government was never elevated enough, and the arena of politics was never large enough to realize their hopes.

Actual and Practical Democracy

The powerful middle-class forces released by the Revolution eventually overwhelmed the high walls of the new federal government, especially under Jefferson's leadership. Despite the Federalists' high hopes, majoritarian factionalism and political parties emerged in the new national arena of politics; indeed, Madison headed one of the parties. And the enterprising people got their paper money after all.

The Philadelphia Convention had rejected Madison's congressional veto over all state laws and replaced it with Article I, Section 10, of the Constitution, which forbade the states from doing certain things, including printing paper money. But the states got around this prohibition by chartering hundreds of banks, which issued the paper money that the American people wanted. And Findley, along with many others of his middling ilk, was not kept out of the Congress. Findley—who, in contrast to the deistic-minded gentry, was a fervent evangelical Christian—entered the Second Congress in 1791 and stayed for so long that in 1817 he was honored by his colleagues as "Father of the House" for being the longest-serving congressman at that point in American history. He was the first congressman to be so honored.

Although many frightened conservatives continued to use the word "democracy" pejoratively (Hamilton—in 1804, on the eve of his fatal duel—called democracy the "real Disease" poisoning the nation), more and more Americans were willing to not only accept but celebrate democracy as the best way of characterizing their political system and their whole society and culture.[68] "The government adopted here is a

DEMOCRACY," the renegade Baptist leader Elias Smith told his fellow Americans in 1809.

> It is well for us to understand this word, so much ridiculed by the international enemies of our beloved country. The word DEMOCRACY is formed of two Greek words, one signifies the people, and the other the government which is in the people. . . . My Friends, let us never be ashamed of DEMOCRACY![69]

By the first decade of the 19th century, most Americans were anything but ashamed of their new egalitarian democracy dominated by ordinary middle-class working people who were much more religious than the elite leaders. America already resembled the kind of democracy that the French visitor Alexis de Tocqueville witnessed two decades later. "After the adoption of the federal constitution," explained noted architect Benjamin Latrobe to the Italian patriot Philip Mazzei in 1806, "the extension of the right of Suffrage in all the states to the majority of all the adult male citizens, planted a germ which has gradually evolved, and has spread actual and practical democracy and political equality over the whole union," which has produced "the greatest sum of happiness that perhaps any nation ever enjoyed."[70]

All the governments—national and state—and in fact the whole society had become dominated by hardworking but *"unlearned"* people. It was hard to find any men of superior talents in government. "The fact is," explained Latrobe, "that superior talents actually excite distrust, and the experience of the world perhaps does not encourage the people to trust men of genius." The society may be prosperous, but the cost of this prosperity has been high. Since most men have to labor for a living, "those arts and refinements, and elegancies which require riches and leisure to their production, are not to be found among the majority of our citizens." Even the rank of gentlemen has been put down in most places by the "unlettered majority," and men of talent exclude themselves from the elective offices of government. "Of this state of society the solid and general advantages are undeniable: but to a cultivated mind, to a man of letters, to a lover of the arts it presents a very unpleasant picture." With everyone in competition to become rich, said Latrobe, "the ties that bind individuals to each other" have become weakened, and the society was in danger of coming apart.[71]

By 1820 a new generation of Americans looked back at the revolutionary generation with awe and wonder and saw in them leaders the likes of which they would never see again. We cannot rely anymore on the views of the revolutionary generation, the Democratic-Republican Martin Van Buren told the New York constitutional convention in 1820. Those who led the Revolution and created the Constitution, he said, were aristocrats, and they had fears of democracy that America's experience had not borne out.[72] Van Buren, who epitomized the new modern party politician, knew that Americans, or at least northern Americans, now lived in a different world, a democratic, middle-class world of ordinary working people whose intense religiosity had to be respected.

This great democracy of the early 19th century was driven by equality, that "great God absolute!" as Herman Melville called it—"the centre and circumference of all democracy." The "Spirit of Equality," he wrote, not only culled the "selectest champions from the kingly commons," but it also brought "democratic dignity" to even "the arm that wields a pick or drives a spike."[73]

Yet the equality of republican citizenship had paradoxical consequences. By the early 19th century in many northern states, free blacks earned the right to vote, and they often were exercising it with particular effectiveness on behalf of those opposed to the Democratic-Republican Party. But black assertions of equality increasingly alarmed many ordinary white people who wanted universal manhood suffrage but not for black citizens. So at the same time that several northern states in the early 19th century did away with any remaining property qualifications on the right of ordinary white citizens to vote, they succumbed to the pressure of white populist majorities and took away the franchise of black citizens—who in some cases had voted for decades. In New York, at the same time as they were taking away the suffrage of longtime black voters, the Democratic-Republicans promoted the illegal voting of Irish immigrants who were not yet citizens, knowing full well which party the newly enfranchised Irish aliens would vote for.

The denial of black participation in the democracy was relentless. No state admitted to the Union after 1819 allowed blacks to vote. By 1840, 93 percent of northern free blacks lived in states that completely or practically excluded them from the suffrage. Since all these examples of racial discrimination, like all assertions of social superiority, violated the egalitarian values of the new democracy, they would inevitably have to be condemned and set right—if the nation were to be made whole and in accord with the principles of its founding. That setting right, which would come at a terrible cost, was unavoidable and essential precisely because the United States really meant to be a democracy.

Despite the many examples of racial injustice, the persistence of slavery in the undemocratic South, and great disparities of wealth in the society—despite all that, within decades following the Declaration of Independence, the United States laid claim to being the most democratic and egalitarian nation in history. It was already by then a unique nation dominated by ordinary, Bible-toting people, violent and obsessed with consuming alcohol and making money, vulgar and vibrant, barbarous and boisterous: the only great democracy in a world of monarchies and one that awed and frightened some of its own citizens and many Europeans. It seemed to represent the future for all of humanity.

Notes

1. "Cain to the People of Pennsylvania: Letter 8," Northern Illinois University Digital Library, https://digital.lib.niu.edu/islandora/object/niu-amarch%3A88192.

2. David Ramsay, "A Dissertation on the Manner of Acquiring the Character and Privileges of a Citizen of the United States," Evans Early American Imprint Collection, 1789, http://name.umdl.umich.edu/N17114.0001.001.

3. Alexander Hamilton, "Second Letter from Phocion, [April 1784]," Founders Online, https://founders.archives.gov/documents/Hamilton/01-03-02-0347.

4. John Adams, *A Defence of the Constitutions of Government of the United States of America* (London: C. Dilly and John Stockdale, 1787), 2:18.

5. John Adams, "VII. To the Inhabitants of the Colony of Massachusetts-Bay," in *Papers of John Adams*, ed. Robert J. Taylor, vol. 2 (Cambridge, MA: Belknap Press, 1977), https://www.masshist.org/publications/adams-papers/index.php/volume/ADMS-06-02.

6. John Adams, "[Notes for an Oration at Braintree, Spring 1772.]," Founders Online, https://founders.archives.gov/documents/Adams/01-02-02-0002-0002-0001.

7. Richard Henry Lee, letter to General Charles Lee, June 29, 1776, in *The Letters of Richard Henry Lee*, ed. James Curtis Ballagh (New York: MacMillan Company, 1911), 1:202, https://archive.org/details/richhenryleeleto1rich rich.

8. Benjamin Rush, "Observations upon the Present Government of Pennsylvania in Four Letters to the People of Pennsylvania," Evans Early American Imprint Collection, 1777, http://name.umdl.umich.edu/N12353.0001.001.

9. James Madison, "Notes for the *National Gazette* Essays, [ca. 19 December 1791–3 March 1792]," Founders Online, https://founders.archives.gov/documents/Madison/01-14-02-0144.

10. Henry Laurens, "Extract of a Letter to the President from H. Laurens," September 10, 1777, in *Documentary History of the American Revolution*, ed. R. W. Gibbes (New York: D. Appleton & Co., 1855), 90–91.

11. Jacob Cuyler, letter to Jeremiah Wadsworth, July 20, 1778, in *To Starve the Army at Pleasure: Continental Army Administration and American Political Culture, 1775–1783*, ed. E. Wayne Carp (Chapel Hill, NC: University of North Carolina Press, 2017), 106.

12. Charles Thomson, "To Thomas Jefferson from Charles Thomson, 6 April 1786," Founders Online, https://founders.archives.gov/documents/Jefferson/01-09-02-0334.

13. David Ramsay, "An Oration on the Advantages of American Independence: Delivered Before a Public Assembly of the Inhabitants of Charlestown, South-Carolina, on the Fourth of July, 1778, the Second Anniversary of That Glorious Aera," Evans Early American Imprint Collection, 1778, https://quod.lib.umich.edu/e/evans/N28767.0001.001.

14. *South-Carolina and American General Gazette*, November 6, 1777, quoted in Gordon S. Wood, *The Creation of the American Republic, 1776–1787* (Chapel Hill, NC: University of North Carolina Press, 2011), 100.

15. *Gazette of the State of South-Carolina*, May 13, April 29, 1784, quoted in Gordon S. Wood, *The Creation of the American Republic, 1776–1787* (Chapel Hill, NC: University of North Carolina Press, 2011), 482–83.

16. James Madison, "Observations on Jefferson's Draft of a Constitution for Virginia, [ca. 15 October] 1788," Founders Online, https://founders.archives.gov/documents/Madison/01-11-02-0216.

17. Ezra Stiles, "The United States Elevated to Glory and Honor," Electronic Texts in American Studies, 1783, https://digitalcommons.unl.edu/etas/41.

18. "The Republican. No. II.," *Connecticut Courant*, February 12, 1787.

19. Max Farrand, ed., *The Records of the Federal Convention of 1787* (New Haven, CT: Yale University Press, 1911), 1:48, https://www.loc.gov/resource/llscdam.llfr001/?st=gallery.

20. Benjamin Thurston, "Address to the Public Containing Some Remarks on the Present Political State of the American Republicks, etc," in *American Political Writing During the Founding Era: 1760–1805*, ed. Charles S. Hyneman and Donald S. Lutz (Indianapolis, IN: Liberty Fund, 1983), 1:644.

21. William Plumer, letter to William Coleman, May 31, 1786, in *Publications of the Colonial Society of Massachusetts: Transaction 1906–1907* (Boston, MA: Colonial Society of Massachusetts, 1910), 11:384, https://www.colonialsociety.org/node/187.

22. Henry Knox, letter to Rufus King, July 15, 1787, in *The Life and Correspondence of Rufus King*, ed. Charles R. King (G. P. Putnam's Sons, 1894), 228.

23. James Madison, letter to Caleb Wallace, August 23, 1785, Founders Online, https://founders.archives.gov/documents/Madison/01-08-02-0184.

24. James Madison, "Vices of the Political System of the United States, April 1787," Founders Online, https://founders.archives.gov/documents/Madison/01-09-02-0187.

25. John Adams, letter to Richard Cranch, July 4, 1786, in *Adams Family Correspondence*, ed. Margaret A. Hogan et al., vol. 7 (Cambridge, MA: Belknap Press, 2005), https://www.masshist.org/publications/adams-papers/index.php/volume/ADMS-04-07.

26. George Washington, letter to George Clinton, April 20, 1785, in *The Writings of George Washington from the Original Manuscript Sources 1745–1799*, ed. John C. Fitzpatrick (Washington, DC: Government Printing Office, 1938), 28:134.

27. George Washington, "From George Washington to John Jay, 18 May 1786," Founders Online, https://founders.archives.gov/documents/Washington/04-04-02-0063.

28. John Adams, "V. to the Inhabitants of the Colony of Massachusetts-Bay," in *Papers of John Adams*, ed. Robert J. Taylor, vol. 2 (Cambridge, MA: Belknap Press, 1977), https://www.masshist.org/publications/adams-papers/index.php/view/ADMS-06-02-02-0072-0006#sn=1.

29. *Federalist*, no. 10 (James Madison), https://avalon.law.yale.edu/18th_century/fed10.asp.

30. James Madison, "Tuesday June 26. in Convention," in *The Writings of James*

Madison, ed. Galliard Hunt (New York: G. P. Putnam's Sons, 1902), 3:288.

31. William Henry Drayton, "Justum, ac propositi virum," *South-Carolina Gazette*, September 21, 1769.

32. William Henry Drayton, "An si atro dente me petiverit," *South-Carolina Gazette*, October 12, 1769.

33. Thomas Gordon and John Trenchard, *Cato's Letters, or Essays on Liberty, Civil and Religious, and Other Important Subjects*, ed. Ronald Hamowy, vol. 3 (Indianapolis, IN: Liberty Fund, 1995), https://oll.libertyfund.org/title/gordon-cato-s-letters-vol-3-march-10-1722-to-december-1-1722-lf-ed.

34. Adam Smith, *An Inquiry into the Nature and Causes of the Wealth of Nations*, ed. R. H. Campbell, A. S. Skinner, and William B. Todd (Carmel, IN: Liberty Fund, 1982), 2:783.

35. Smith, *An Inquiry into the Nature and Causes of the Wealth of Nations*, 1:265.

36. John Dickinson and Richard Henry Lee, *Empire and Nation: Letters from a Farmer in Pennsylvania; Letters from the Federal Farmer*, ed. Forrest McDonald (Indianapolis, IN: Liberty Fund, 1962).

37. Richard Jackson, letter to Benjamin Franklin, June 17, 1755, Founders Online, https://founders.archives.gov/documents/Franklin/01-06-02-0043.

38. George Clymer, letter to Thomas FitzSimons, May 24, 1783, in Jerry Grundfest, "George Clymer, Philadelphia Revolutionary, 1739–1813," (PhD diss., Columbia University, 1973), 165.

39. Robert R. Livingston, letter to John Rutledge, October 10, 1776, in *The Democratic Republicans of New York: The Origins, 1763–1797*, ed. Alfred E. Young (Chapel Hill, NC: University of North Carolina Press, 1967), 27.

40. H. H. Brackenridge, *Modern Chivalry: Containing the Adventures of a Captain and Teague O'Regan, His Servant* (Pittsburgh, PA: R. Patterson & Lambdin, 1819), 205.

41. Gordon S. Wood, "The Origins of American Democracy, or How the People Became Judges in Their Own Causes, the Sixty-Ninth Cleveland-Marshall Fund Lecture," *Cleveland State Law Review* 47, no. 3 (1999): 320, https://engagedscholarship.csuohio.edu/clevstlrev/vol47/iss3/3.

42. Matthew Carey, ed., *Debate and Proceedings of the General Assembly of Pennsylvania* (1786; Ann Arbor, MI: Evans Early American Imprint Collection), 72, https://quod.lib.umich.edu/cgi/t/text/text-idx?c=evans;idno=N15592.0001.001.

43. Carey, ed., *Debate and Proceedings of the General Assembly of Pennsylvania*.

44. *Federalist*, no. 10 (Madison).

45. James Madison, letter to George Washington, April 16, 1787, Founders Online, https://founders.archives.gov/documents/Madison/01-09-02-0208.

46. James Winthrop, "Agrippa XV," Teaching American History, January 29, 1788, https://teachingamericanhistory.org/document/agrippa-xv.

47. James Madison, letter to Thomas Jefferson, New York, October 24, 1787, Founders Online, https://founders.archives.gov/documents/Jefferson/01-12-02-0274.

48. *Federalist*, no. 10 (Madison).

49. "Popular Election of the First Branch of the Legislature, [31 May] 1787," Founders Online, https://founders.archives.gov/documents/Madison/01-10-02-0008.

50. James Madison, "Vices of the Political System of the United States, April 1787," Founders Online, https://founders.archives.gov/documents/Madison/01-09-02-0187.

51. Benjamin Workman, "Philadelphiensis IX," Teaching American History, February 6, 1788, https://teachingamericanhistory.org/document/philadelphiensis-ix.

52. Melancton Smith, "New York Ratifying Convention," Founders' Constitution, June 20–21, 1788, http://press-pubs.uchicago.edu/founders/documents/v1ch13s37.html.

53. Herbert J. Storing, ed., *The Complete Anti-Federalist* (Chicago: University of Chicago Press, 1981), 2:236.

54. Storing, ed., *The Complete Anti-Federalist*, 230.

55. Richard Henry Lee, letter to Edmund Randolph, October 16, 1787, Lee Family Digital Archive, https://leefamilyarchive.org/history-papers-letters-transcripts-ballagh-b368.

56. Samuel Chase, quoted in Philip A. Crowl, "Anti-Federalism in Maryland, 1787–1788," *William and Mary Quarterly* 4, no. 4 (October 1947): 464.

57. Louis Otto, letter to Comte de Vergennes, October 10, 1786, in Gordon S. Wood, *The Creation of the American Republic, 1776–1787* (Chapel Hill, NC: University of North Carolina Press, 1969), 495.

58. Crowl, "Anti-Federalism in Maryland," 464.

59. Richard Walsh, *Charleston's Sons of Liberty: A Study of the Artisans, 1763–1789* (Columbia, SC: University of South Carolina Press, 1959), 132.

60. Storing, ed., *The Complete Anti-Federalist*, 230.

61. *Federalist*, no. 35 (Alexander Hamilton), https://avalon.law.yale.edu/18th_century/fed35.asp.

62. James Wilson, *Collected Work of James Wilson*, ed. Kermit L. Hall and Mark David Hall, vol. 2 (Indianapolis, IN: Liberty Fund, 2007), https://oll.libertyfund.org/title/garrison-collected-works-of-james-wilson-vol-2.

63. *Federalist*, no. 58 (James Madison), https://avalon.law.yale.edu/18th_century/fed58.asp.

64. *Federalist*, no. 46 (James Madison), https://avalon.law.yale.edu/18th_century/fed46.asp.

65. John Bach McMaster and Frederick D. Stone, eds., *Pennsylvania and the Federal Constitution, 1787–1788* (Lancaster, PA: Inquirer Printing, 1888), 223; and Jonathan Elliot, ed., *The Debates in the Several State Conventions on the Adoption of the Federal Constitution, as Recommended by the General Convention at Philadelphia, in 1787. Together with the Journal of the Federal Convention, Luther Martin's Letter, Yates's Minutes, Congressional Opinions, Virginia and Kentucky Resolutions of '98–'99, and Other Illustrations of the Constitution* (Philadelphia, PA: J. B. Lippincott, 1881), 2:424.

66. *Federalist*, no. 63 (James Madison), https://avalon.law.yale.edu/18th_century/fed63.asp.

67. John Stevens, *Observations on Government, Including Some Animadversions on Mr. Adams's Defence of the Constitutions of Government of the United States of America: and on Mr. De Lolme's Constitution of England. By a Farmer, of New-Jersey.* (New York: W. Ross, 1787), 52.

68. Alexander Hamilton, "From Alexander Hamilton to Theodore Sedgwick, 10 July 1804," Founders Online, https://founders.archives.gov/documents/Hamilton/01-26-02-0001-0264.

69. Elias Smith, *The Loving Kindness of God Disposed in the Triumph of Republicanism in America* (n.p.: 1809), quoted in Gordon S. Wood, *Empire of Liberty: A History of the Early Republic, 1789–1815* (Oxford, UK: Oxford University Press, 2009), 718.

70. Benjamin Latrobe, letter to Philip Mazzei, December 19, 1806, in Gordon S. Wood, *The Radicalism of the American Revolution* (New York: Vintage Books, 1993), 294–95.

71. Latrobe, letter to Mazzei.

72. Merrill D. Peterson, ed., *Democracy, Liberty, and Property: The State Constitutional Conventions of the 1820s* (New York: Bobbs-Merrill Company, 1966), 206–14.

73. Herman Melville, *Moby Dick; or, The Whale* (New York: Harper & Brothers, 1851), 128.

2

The Spirit of Independence and the Rhythm of Democratic Politics

BRYAN GARSTEN

It is only natural to wonder, after 250 years, how long the American republic will last. While we may sometimes imagine the possibility of a "perpetual republic,"[1] the most reliable prediction about any country—or about any state of affairs—is the one Abraham Lincoln grappled with at the end of a speech in Wisconsin in 1859: "This, too, shall pass away."[2] It is doubtful that our country has finally discovered an escape from that ultimate fate.

Still, even if we begin with the fatalistic insight that our nation is mortal, there is room for us to wonder where in its life cycle we find ourselves today. Were the United States to last as long as ancient Sparta, for example, the 250th anniversary of its independence would mark less than half its lifespan. It is possible that future historians will regard our time, with all its political struggles and disappointments, as merely one crisis among many, perhaps as the last part of the first working out of the principles of the founding.

"There is consolation in the thought that America is young," said Frederick Douglass at a July Fourth celebration in 1852.[3] At that point the country was just 76 years old, but it must have seemed to many observers that the American experiment was already nearing its end. The republic had failed to realize its founding ideals and was foundering on a deep sectional divide. Despite that, Douglass, a former slave who had experienced the country's most profound failure firsthand, asked his audience to imagine a longer future for the country. Can we ask the same of ourselves today?

Imagining a longer future for a democratic United States seems more plausible if we rediscover a feature of democracies that was at one time familiar but is now less often noted—the tendency to fall into cycles of institutional dysfunction and popular discontent, followed by reform. There is a certain *rhythm* to democratic politics.[4] There are fits and starts, falls into corruption followed by recoveries. There is no guarantee of recovery, of course—the rhythm offers us no justification for complacency. But there is, still, the possibility of an upswing, if we can find our way toward it.

What drives these cycles? In this chapter, I would like to draw attention to the *spirit of independence*. Theorists of democracy, focused on the importance of equality, solidarity, and mutual interdependence, sometimes imagine they can live without this potentially dangerous sentiment. They forget that the democratic world they live in would never have been established without it, and they too often ignore the ways that both elites and democratic majorities can spark new bursts of that spirit as a reaction to their overzealous rule.

Libertarians, on the other hand, tend to forget that the spirit of independence is and ought to be an *episodic* passion, at least as a dominant force in our national life. It rouses us periodically to protect ourselves and keep our rulers decent, but it does not suffice for stable rule or fair politics. Neither solidarists nor libertarians situate the spirit of independence within the rhythm of democratic politics. They evaluate the passion for independence, either positively or negatively, as if it were a steady demand rather than a periodic rising up.

The Declaration of Independence is the exemplary American articulation of this spirit. Both Thomas Jefferson, its principal author, and Lincoln, its most important interpreter, assumed that republics tend to decay but can also be renewed. The tendency toward corruption, which spurs declarations of independence in response, produces the rhythm I mean to highlight. In looking for a way to *manage* this rhythm, we find ourselves rediscovering an important purpose for a constitution.

The Spirit of Independence and Its Sources

Perhaps some people have a natural desire to rule, but many of us tend to find the actual experience of having authority to be more trouble than it is worth. If there were an effortless way to have the world conform to our wishes, few of us would be able to resist the temptation. The actual work of ruling over others, however, embroils us in all the messiness of managing other human beings, defending ourselves against rivals, compensating for the jealousies that our power necessarily excites, and maintaining loyalty among our advisers. Ruling over others is work, and most of us will find, especially as we age, that laziness or exhaustion saps our political ambition. A political system designed on the assumption that we all want to rule overestimates our vigor.

The opposite inclination—the wish to relax into a carefree and secure state of being protected and cared for—is more attractive than many of us like to admit. Provided that we are ruled by a wise and benevolent ruler, someone attuned to our interests and experienced enough to know how to properly watch over us, the thought of being cared for is not unattractive. Democratic instincts may not allow us to concede ultimate authority to any particular person or class of persons, but as long as we imagine a set of officials or an intelligent algorithm merely executing the judgments of an abstract "public opinion," we may find we can easily reconcile ourselves to a happy passivity. Public opinion is our own opinion, after all, even if we do not bear much responsibility for its content. The vague sense that we somehow participate in public opinion compensates us for the extent to which we let ourselves be ruled by it.

Those two different inclinations, to rule and to let ourselves be ruled, might seem to exhaust the set of possible orientations toward rule, but the spirit of independence is distinct from both. The spirit of independence can be fierce when it erupts but is not often sustained for long. It does not initiate action but is, instead, fundamentally reactive. We feel this spirit when we bristle at rule imposed unfairly, carelessly, or clumsily. This is the indignation that propels us to take to the streets to demonstrate against the latest outrage, though if we then retire home happy at having expressed ourselves, we reveal how quickly it can fade.

A stronger version of the independent spirit propels the people who fight in revolutionary wars and, in a different way, those who flee oppressive regimes. Revolutionaries and refugees both crave independence, often in bursts of determination. If they are successful in breaking free, they soon find themselves in a new political situation wondering how to replace the institutions and practices that had structured their old lives. The spirit of independence is not especially helpful in this next task. It has played its part, fueling the takeoff from the planet's surface, but the rest of the journey must rely on other power sources.

We might think, therefore, that the spirit of independence should be firmly limited to moments of liberation. Perhaps it was necessary at the nation's founding to free us from the British or even, more grandly, from the vestiges of the premodern European world, with its inherited rights to rule, claims of divine right, and priestly domination. Having done its work, should this spirit not then be safely confined to the past, where it cannot disturb the fragile peace of our now established constitutional regime? Decent as it eventually aimed to be, however, this regime could not help but accumulate grievances as it gathered power for itself and drifted into corruption. And in its founding period, the American regime never allowed the spirit of independence of the enslaved portion of the population to do its work in the first place. There was work for the spirit of independence to do even after the founding.

Even before the Declaration of Independence, international observers had noticed a distinctively independent spirit in the American character. Edmund Burke, the British statesman who argued for reconciliation with the American colonies during the immediate prerevolutionary period, analyzed this attitude in a 1775 speech. He pointed to six historical sources that came together to produce an unusually strong passion for independence in Americans, including their descent from Englishmen with a tradition of resistance to taxation by centralized authorities and, importantly, the strength of Protestant separatism in the northern colonies.[5]

In the past half century, scholars have drawn our attention to republican or "neo-Roman" writings against dependence on the arbitrary will of another.[6] Burke reminds us that the connotations around the word "independence" had also been shaped, more strongly than we sometimes remember, by its use in discussions of church authority. The word had become common only during the 17th century in England, when it referred to Protestant churches that refused to subordinate themselves to any central ecclesiastical authority such as Rome, the Anglican Church, or even Presbyterian governing bodies.

The Independents thought each congregation should stand on its own feet and govern itself, often in a more or less democratic fashion. In England, the Independents gained control during the civil war of the mid-1600s, with Oliver Cromwell's New Model Army, and they expelled their enemies to gain control of Parliament. Eventually, they put King Charles I to death and declared a commonwealth. With the restoration of the Stuart monarchy in 1660, however, the Independents were forced out, and some fled to America. In New England, the Independents were also known as Congregationalists, since they insisted that each congregation choose its own pastors and govern its own affairs.

For a sense of American Independent political thought, we could turn to figures such as John Wise, a prominent prerevolution minister from Ipswich, Massachusetts. Wise gained fame early in the century for his pamphlets opposing Increase Mather, an elite Boston minister who had tried to impose a Presbyterian sort of institutional oversight on the churches of the region. Wise bristled at efforts to impose centralized ecclesiastical authority, and he wrote forcefully against measures by the British colonial administration to impose taxes. In his day, there was no clear line between church matters and political affairs, and some scholars have found in Wise a lost "father" of the American Revolution. While I would not want to overstate his prescience or suggest, anachronistically, that he endorsed political democracy, he did articulate key ideas that would later appear in the Declaration of Independence.[7] We can hear, in his writing, the sort of prickly independence that observers like Burke identified as a distinctly American spirit.

Among the sources of the American spirit of independence that Burke left out was the example that Native American societies offered to the colonists during more than a century of uneasy coexistence, shifting alliances, and wars before the Revolution. When Burke noticed, with surprise, that the former colonists of Massachusetts had been able to govern themselves even in the absence of English authorities, he remarked that "anarchy is found tolerable."[8] One impetus to explore the possibility of "anarchic" self-government had come from seeing how the Indigenous tribes engaged in self-rule. Even as Independent ministers such as John Eliot and Roger Williams worked to convert those tribes to Christianity, they also learned the Native languages and sought to understand their point of view.

Impressed by the contempt the Natives had for the hierarchies and submissions of European society and admiring the happiness the tribes seemed to produce in everyday life, some colonists found themselves wondering whether a greater degree of independence, what had seemed in Europe a dangerous anarchism, might in fact be an antidote to the vices of European culture and politics. Interestingly, Williams and some of the other Independents most interested in the Native societies returned to England during the English Civil War and were influential in the circles close to Cromwell before returning to the colonies.[9] When we speak about the influence of the Separatists and Puritans of the English Civil War on the New England mind, we should allow that those sects may themselves have already been influenced by the Native American mind. What later European or British observers described as a distinctly American spirit of independence may have represented a conjunction of Indigenous American and English Independent spirits.

Jefferson, first author of the Declaration—and no consistent friend to the Native population—nevertheless indicated how deeply the example of their independence had impressed him and how important he thought it was to preserve a similar spirit in the population of the new United States. Consider a letter he wrote in 1787 to Col. Edward Carrington:

> I am convinced that the societies (as they Indians) which live without government, enjoy in their general mass an infinitely greater degree of happiness than those who live under the European governments. Among the former, public opinion is in the place of law, and restrains morals as powerfully as laws ever did anywhere. Among the latter, under pretense of governing, they have divided their nations into two classes, wolves and sheep. I do not exaggerate. This is a true picture of Europe. Cherish, therefore, that spirit of our people, and keep alive their attention. Do not be too severe upon their errors, but reclaim them by enlightening them. If once they become inattentive to the public affairs, you and I, and Congress and assemblies, Judges and Governors, shall all become wolves. It seems to be the law of our general nature, in spite of individual exceptions; and experience declares that man is the only animal which devours his own kind; for I can apply no milder term to the governments of Europe, and to the general prey of the rich on the poor.[10]

Of course, Jefferson never suggested that the United States should truly emulate Native societies in going "without government." He did not know those societies well, and in the end, his presidency contributed mightily to their conquest, but he did see the proud independence of Indigenous societies as a reminder of the spirit that could fuel resistance to the corruptions of European politics.

Fifty years after the Declaration, Jefferson wrote in a now-famous letter that the document had served as "the signal of arousing men to burst the chains under which monkish ignorance and superstition had persuaded them to bind themselves, and to assume the blessings and security of self-government."[11] His argument was for an episodic rather than a constant eruption of this spirit. To make that possible, it was necessary to preserve the spirit in reserve, as a weapon against lethargy and servitude. The spirit of independence, always under the surface, would burst forth on occasion to protect against the otherwise inevitable tendency for rulers to become, in his language, wolves. Slides into decadence and tyranny, and reactions against these slides, follow one another with a certain regularity, according to Jefferson's understanding of history. This helps explain his famous statements suggesting that no generation should bind the next and that occasional revolutions should be welcomed.[12] In these remarks, we begin to sense the rhythm of politics that the spirit of independence helps produce.

Independence, Equality, and Peoplehood

Today, the Declaration of Independence is most often cited for its statement that all men are created equal. What is the relation between natural equality and the spirit of independence?

Some scholars adopt a deflationary reading of the Declaration, in which the ideas of national independence and separation eclipse that of equality among individuals. Against the rhetorical efforts of Lincoln, Elizabeth Cady Stanton, Martin Luther King Jr., and other reformers to find in the Declaration an inspiration for contemporary civil rights, these scholars emphasize that the document was meant only to justify the separation from Great Britain. The Stanford historian Jack Rakove has argued, for instance, that the famous statement that "all men are created equal" was meant to show only that the American people were naturally equal to the British people in their right to establish a government for themselves.[13] Kermit Roosevelt III, a law professor, has gone further, suggesting that later efforts to enlist the Declaration into movements for civil equality require a forced reading of the Declaration. He suggests giving up on viewing the document as any sort of inspiration for us today.[14] On the deflationary view, to acknowledge the importance of national independence is to de-emphasize the importance of individual equality.

It is striking to notice how faithfully this interpretation echoes the readings of the Declaration advanced by some 19th-century apologists for slavery. Stephen Douglas, for example, whose campaign debates with Lincoln over an Illinois Senate seat raised fundamental matters of principle, argued as well that the Declaration had aimed merely to assert the equal status of American colonists to the British people:

> That [the Declaration's authors] were speaking of British subjects on this continent being equal to British subjects born and residing in Great Britain—that they were entitled to the same inalienable rights, and among them were enumerated life, liberty, and the pursuit of happiness. The declaration was adopted for the purpose of justifying the colonists, in the eyes of the civilized world, in withdrawing their allegiance from the British crown, and dissolving their connection with the mother country.[15]

For Douglas, as for some recent writers, the fact that the document aimed at national independence should cure us of our misguided effort to find in it a basis for the equality of individuals.

Even theorists who admire the Declaration are sometimes uncertain how to understand the apparent gap between its assertion of national independence and the equality of individuals that later activists tried to find in it: "The conceptual tie between the independent person and the independent group, if any, is hardly obvious," writes political theorist George Kateb.[16]

But we can find this conceptual tie if we follow the logical flow of the Declaration's argument closely and notice how both independence and equality are invoked to explain the possibility of creating an entirely new *people*. In speaking of the Americans and the British as two peoples rather than one, the Declaration was insisting to the world that the conflict was not merely a civil war among the British. The question arises, however, of how the colonists had become a separate people. What made it possible, conceivable, for one people to split in this way? What is "a people," anyway?

The traditional view of "a people" is that its members are tied by blood, territory, or long-shared history and culture. On this view, our ancestors, our habits and traditions, our way of life—all constitute us at such a deep level that our very identities cannot be understood or explained without reference to our membership and shared inheritances. Membership and inheritance, in turn, take the form of finding our place in the structure of the people we are born into—for instance, within the family structures, ecclesiastical orders, or ways of dividing up work into guilds. These structures are hierarchies of various kinds. If we accept this definition, no one can simply *decide* not to be a member of a people. My very identity is bound up with my role in the social structure of the people I am born into. I am what I am, whether I am happy about it or not. There would be something willful and blind, a kind of self-deception, in simply *asserting* that I am no longer what I, by any reasonable analysis, have always been. If peoplehood is part of who I am, I can no more leave it behind than I can remove my skin.

If, however, peoplehood is not an intrinsic part of me but instead a choice—if peoplehood can come about through a political act of institution or the practice of governing together—then it would make sense to assert that a new people can be created in the way the Declaration suggests. But peoplehood can come about through choice only if individuals are not existentially constituted by the social structures they were born into. We can declare independence from one people only if each of us is not naturally subject to that people or any part of it. To insist on this fact is to insist that we are naturally equals.

Jefferson's original rough draft of the Declaration apparently asserted that all men are born "equal and independent."[7] These two attributes, equality and independence, must have been linked together in his mind, understood as related descriptors of human beings who are, *by nature*, at liberty to engage in the work of creating a new people together. The Declaration's famous assertion that "all men are created equal" appears in its second paragraph as a crucial premise in an argument about how a new people might come into existence. The new independence of a nation presumes the creation of a people, which in turn assumes the equality and independence of its members.

Americans had gradually created a new people by living together and developing habits of self-government in the colonies during the decades between settlement and the revolution. Since the relationship of peoplehood had developed among them, they could now act together, even without the government, to create a new one. The Declaration announced the culmination of that process and put forward a view of political thought that explained how such a thing as a new people could come about—a new people who could not have developed unless the individuals living in the colonies had been naturally equal and independent, existentially free to develop new ties of peoplehood.

Here again, we can find implicit in the Declaration's political thought a set of assumptions about the rhythm of politics: Peoples begin to form slowly, as they experience a shared political situation over time, but they can then coalesce and become conscious of themselves in a rush, as they come up against outside efforts to rule them. At those moments, a new consciousness of independence emerges, and a spirited self-assertion is required. It was "necessary," the Declaration insisted, for the colonists to make this declaration. The situation had ripened; the "course of events" had brought them to this moment and "impelled" them to take a stand. The necessity had not always existed; the Americans were not late to a tea party. There was a pace to the growth of peoplehood, and there was a right moment, a kairos, for the colonists to declare the existence of this new people to the world and, indeed, to themselves.

The "Future Use" of the Declaration

If the conceptual tie between the spirit of independence and equality is forgotten—if the Declaration is read as merely a justification for a separation from the British government—the relevance of the document for future generations is unclear. Lincoln therefore resisted Douglass's deflationary reading of the Declaration. Instead, he revived and deepened a Jeffersonian view of the document and its potential role in the life cycle of the republic.

Lincoln preferred that swings toward anarchy or tyranny could be contained in a constitutional framework. He did not succumb to Jefferson's occasional enthusiasm for bloody revolutions, but he did imagine the need for periodic renewals, moments when he thought the Declaration could play an important role. Within that framework, Lincoln did more to make the Declaration central to American unity than anyone else, turning what had been a partisan rallying cry for the Jeffersonian Republican Party against the Federalists into a touchstone for the whole union.[18]

If separation from England was the Declaration's only purpose, Lincoln argued, then the document was of merely historical interest and "of no practical use now—mere rubbish—old wadding left to rot on the battle-field after the victory is won." The yearly celebrations of the Fourth of July would be meaningless if Douglas was correct about how to read the Declaration. Lincoln responded to Douglas's interpretation with sarcasm:

> I understand you are preparing to celebrate the "Fourth," tomorrow week. What for? The doings of that day had no reference to the present; and quite half of you are not even descendants of those who were referred to at that day. But I suppose you will celebrate; and will even go so far as to read the Declaration. Suppose after you read it once in the old fashioned way, you read it once more with Judge Douglas' version. It will then

run thus: "We hold these truths to be self-evident that all British subjects who were on this continent eighty-one years ago, were created equal to all British subjects born and *then* residing in Great Britain."

And now I appeal to all—to Democrats as well as others—are you really willing that the Declaration shall be thus frittered away?—thus left no more at most, than an interesting memorial of the dead past? thus shorn of vitality, and practical value; and left without the *germ* or even the *suggestion* of the individual rights of man in it?[19] (Emphasis in original.)

Lincoln proposed a different reading of the Declaration that would make it more than a yearly occasion for fireworks. He hoped the inspiration of the Declaration would be useful at key moments in the nation's future, when rulers succumbed to tyrannical temptations or when a corruption of public sentiments crept into the political culture. The Declaration's authors had looked ahead, Lincoln suggested, and had seen that as the country aged away from its revolutionary founding era, it would tend, as all republics did, to decay. They had put the statement of equality into the Declaration as an obstacle to future tyrants:

Its authors meant it to be, thank God, it is now proving itself, a stumbling block to those who in after times might seek to turn a free people back into the hateful paths of despotism. They knew the proneness of prosperity to breed tyrants, and they meant when such should re-appear in this fair land and commence their vocation they should find left for them at least one hard nut to crack.[20]

Lincoln is sometimes read as though he believed in the gradual realization of the principles of equality. That formulation, however, leaves out an important component of his views about slavery's place in the national story. Lincoln did not think of slavery as a problem that the founders had merely left unresolved. He thought it was a problem that had *worsened* since the founding.

The deepening entrenchment of slavery into the country's economic and social structures seemed to him an example of a more general tendency for the republic to fall away from its original commitment to freedom. In 1855, he wrote a telling short letter to George Robertson, an older Kentucky lawyer who had shared his hopes of gradual emancipation for enslaved Americans. Lincoln indicated that his own hopes for gradual emancipation had faded; the tsar of Russia would be more likely to step down and create a republic there, Lincoln remarked, than American slave owners would be ready to free their slaves. He understood this to be a new development. In the days of the revolution, he noted, many states had freed their slaves in a burst of revolutionary spirit. With the passage of time, that spirit had diminished:

> On the question of liberty, as a principle, we are not what we have been. When we were the political slaves of King George, and wanted to be free, we called the maxim that "all men are created equal" a self evident truth; but now when we have grown fat, and have lost all dread of being slaves ourselves, we have become so greedy to be *masters* that we call the same maxim "a self evident lie." The fourth of July has not quite dwindled away; it is still a great day—*for burning fire-crackers!!!*[21] (Emphasis in original.)

With this danger in mind—that after a time "we are not what we have been"—Lincoln expressed hope that the Declaration might serve as a standard and a spur. He would later repeat and elaborate his claim that the prejudice against the black population was worse in his time than it had been during the founding period. He was also aware of the tendency to naturalize existing inequalities—and even of the developing science of racism that Confederate Vice President Alexander Stephens would

THE SPIRIT OF INDEPENDENCE 55

invoke in the famous "Cornerstone" speech of 1861. Against Chief Justice
Roger B. Taney, Douglas, and others who denied that the Declaration's
statement of equality was intended to include enslaved people, Lincoln
argued that the founders had intended the basic rights of life, liberty, and
the pursuit of happiness to apply to all as a standard for the future:

> [The founders] meant simply to declare the *right*, so that the
> *enforcement* of it might follow as fast [as] circumstances should
> permit. They meant to set up a standard maxim for free society,
> which should be familiar to all, and revered by all; constantly
> looked to, constantly labored for, and even though never per-
> fectly attained, constantly approximated, and thereby con-
> stantly spreading and deepening its influence, and augmenting
> the happiness and value of life to all people of all colors every-
> where. The assertion that "all men are created equal" was of
> no practical use in effecting our separation from Great Britain;
> and it was placed in the Declaration, not for that, but *for future
> use*.[22] (Emphasis added.)

To imagine a future use for the principle of natural equality was to
imagine a politics that required the periodic reassertion of the principle
against tendencies leading in the opposite direction. The "unfinished
work" that Lincoln emphasized in his most famous speeches included
responding to the periodic drift into corruption—the fact that "we have
grown fat" and are tempted by the attractions of mastery, "the proneness
of prosperity to breed tyrants" not just among elected leaders but among
the people themselves. Against those dangers, the Declaration could serve as
"a stumbling block" and "one hard nut to crack."[23]

Lincoln used the phrase "the individual rights of man" to describe what
Douglas's deflationary reading of the Declaration would sacrifice. That he
understood the Declaration's assertion of natural equality in the language
of *rights* shows another link between equality and the spirit of independence. A right is a domain of action that we feel to be ours and so will be

more likely to defend, the borders of which we will patrol vigilantly. To think of equality in terms of rights is to harness the spirit of independence: We rise up in indignation when someone trespasses on our rights. Of course, we may also rise up to defend the rights of others, but the core appeal of rights is the spirited self-defense that they arouse. Even when we stand up for others, we do so in part because we are somehow offended on their behalf by the violation's implied insult.

Lincoln's consequential effort to find in the Declaration a resource "for future use" updated Jefferson's notion that "the spirit of '76" would be needed at key moments in the life of the republic as part of the pattern of its politics. John Stuart Mill, observing the American Civil War from England, wrote that while war is always lamentable, this war, waged on a matter of principle and against an institution so obviously tyrannical, was the sort that could be "a means to [the Americans'] regeneration."[24] Republics need such regeneration from time to time; that is their rhythm.

The Natural Conservatism of the People

Jefferson and Lincoln sought to maintain the spirit of independence in reserve and encouraged it to swell up periodically to renew the project of republican self-government. Others, however, have seen in this spirit a dangerous enticement to dissatisfaction and rebellion. Jonathan Boucher, a Tory writing in the years leading up to the revolution, saw the disruptive potential of John Locke's political principles even before Jefferson had applied them:

> Any attempt, therefore, to introduce this fantastic system into practice, would reduce the whole business of social life to the wearisome, confused, and useless talk of mankind's first expressing, and then withdrawing, their consent to an endless succession of schemes of government. Governments, though always forming, would never be completely formed:

for, the majority to-day, might be the minority to-morrow; and, of course, that which is now fixed might and would be soon unfixed.[25]

Unleashing the spirit of independence, therefore, "can produce only perpetual dissensions and contests, and bring back mankind to a supposed state of nature; arming every man's hand, like Ishmael's, against every man, and rendering the world an *aceldama*, or field of blood."[26] (Emphasis in original.)

In the middle of the 20th century, some conservative intellectuals blamed Lincoln for having made such a dangerous principle central to the nation's self-understanding by emphasizing the importance of the Declaration. According to M. E. Bradford, for instance,

Lincoln's "second founding" is fraught with peril and carries with it the prospect of an endless series of turmoils and revolutions, all dedicated to freshly discovered meanings of equality as a "proposition." . . . And its full potential for mischief is yet to be determined.[27]

Bradford and others thought the seeds of rebellion could be found especially in a single word in the Declaration: The natural rights to life, liberty, and the pursuit of happiness were said to be "unalienable." They could not be given away. This meant that the people would always remain watchful, surveilling, and jealous of their rights. The Declaration's theory of consent seemed to encourage a politics of disorder.

We should not dismiss this concern too quickly, because it helps us read the Declaration from a fresh perspective. We have read the opening words so many times that we have become numb to their disruptive and violent implications. The right to make war against our government when we are dissatisfied with it, with the hope of setting up something entirely new in its place—how could this possibility not disturb our sleep if we took it seriously? After all, who is really satisfied with the government we have? Governing is difficult work, and even modest success by government tends to produce dissatisfaction.

We believe we deserve justice, so we are not especially grateful when the government treats us as it should. But we are exquisitely sensitive to every failure, and when the inevitable mistakes pile up over time, so do our resentments. Governments have much of the power in society, and so they attract much of the blame for social ills. In the 1790s, early in the American experiment, it was common for disaffected leaders, frustrated with political developments, to threaten to leave the union altogether. "When reading the history of these years," writes one political theorist, "it sometimes seems as if every major political event . . . caused one group or another to threaten the breakup of the union."[28]

Political leaders have historically tried to balance against this danger by instilling patience, loyalty, obedience, and patriotism in their peoples. Even Locke had articulated a notion of "tacit" consent that diminished the unsettling implications of his theory, arguing that even if we have not explicitly agreed to our government, we implicitly consent to it simply by living under its laws and accepting the benefits it provides; even someone merely passing through a country agrees to its laws by virtue of using the public roads. When Jefferson drafted the Declaration, he did not mention tacit consent and declined to moderate the implications of the consent principle with Locke's caveat. The unrestricted principle of consent adopted by the Declaration thus upset what a long tradition of political thought had regarded as a delicate balance. It seemed to recklessly encourage our tendency toward righteous indignation.

Jefferson did include, however, a different line of argument by which Locke had mitigated the anarchic effect of his thought. Locke had disputed a foundational assumption about human nature that the monarchists seemed to endorse—the assumption that people would tend to dissolve governments if given a chance to act on their frustrations. Boucher, the Tory writer, articulated this assumption clearly in explaining his opposition to Lockean principles:

As the people, in all circumstances, but more especially when trained to make and unmake governments, are at least as well disposed to do the latter as the former, it is morally impossible that there should be any thing like permanency or stability in a government so formed.[29] (Emphasis added.)

Boucher's assumption was that people would naturally tend in the direction of "unmaking" governments. Against that premise, Jefferson asserted in the Declaration that "all experience hath shewn, that mankind are more disposed to suffer, while evils are sufferable, than to right themselves by abolishing the forms to which they are accustomed."

Jefferson drew this idea directly from Locke's *Second Treatise of Civil Government*, which assured its readers that "the People . . . are more disposed to suffer, than right themselves by Resistance" and that "People are not so easily got out of their old forms as some are apt to suggest."[30] What Locke and Jefferson insist on is that the people—the primary agent in republican politics and the drivers of any revolution—are a habitually *conservative* force in politics. They tend to want to continue living as they have been, even in the face of ordinary dissatisfactions. Only when abuses have piled up for a long time can they be aroused to resistance. Even then, it will take a coordinated effort by leaders willing to risk their "Lives, [their] Fortunes and [their] sacred Honor" to stir them to action.

It is always a fundamental question in politics how to navigate between the dangers of anarchy and tyranny. If the natural human tendency is to suffer abuse rather than rebel at every imposition, then the danger of tyranny seems, in general, to be greater than that of anarchy, and the spirit of independence, even with the instability it threatens, will seem less a poison and more an antidote. Critics of the Declaration's principles, such as Boucher and Bradford, imagined that the spirit of independence would be unleashed more or less continually, leading us to constantly unsettle our inheritances in pursuit of an elusive, abstract, and ultimately unreachable vision of perfection. The theory of politics in the Declaration, however, rests on the idea that these critics overestimate our restlessness and underestimate our attachment to the way things are. There is a spirit of independence, but it makes its appearance in politics episodically rather than constantly undermining authority and stability.

The Declaration's assumptions about the ordinary conservatism of the people can be traced back to the complicated republicanism of Niccolò Machiavelli, who thought most people's fundamental political impulse was not the desire to rule but the demand not to *be* ruled. The corresponding rhythm of political life that Machiavelli described in his account of ancient Rome—a rhythm composed of falls into corruption punctuated by refoundings—is closely related to the one implicit in the Declaration. But the ancient renewals Machiavelli described had been spectacular, violent affairs. Could the leaders of a republic tame this rhythm, harnessing its energy to public purposes and releasing its excesses in ways that would minimize the damage done? That question remains a live one for Americans celebrating the Declaration of Independence today.[31]

Constitutionalizing the Spirit of Independence

If the Declaration assumes that people are generally willing to suffer "a long train of abuses" until it is time to act, it also assumes that it is, in fact, possible for us to create new political forms together. Our creative political power is presumed in the assertion of our right to institute new governments:

> It is the Right of the People to alter or to abolish [the government], and to institute new Government, laying its foundation on such principles and organizing its powers in such form, as to them shall seem most likely to effect their Safety and Happiness.

If a long record of suffering is the rule but casting off governments and creating new ones a possibility, then the full cycle of politics implicit in the Declaration comes to light. The document seems to suppose at least three different phases of politics: Ordinarily, we live under a government and perhaps suffer under it, drifting into almost inevitable periods of corruption. The possibility of escape from these periods leads us to pay attention and perhaps, during bad periods, to imagine something better. The mere possibility of escape opens the door for leaders to spur us into reform or revolution, but our tendency to stay in existing forms also makes their task a difficult one. If the leaders succeed in rousing us, however, they move us into the second mode of politics: the work of abolishing the old forms. If they are successful at that, as well, a third phase of politics remains—building the new institutions that will hopefully serve us well for a time, until they, too, inevitably drift astray.

If this rhythm is implicit in the Declaration, and if Lincoln understood that, then his famous effort to place the Declaration at the heart of an American political religion emphasizing obedience to the laws should be understood as an effort to integrate the spirit of independence into a constitutional regime, to turn the potentially disruptive Jeffersonian "spirit of '76" into a strength of the system.[32] At the moment of greatest danger to the republic, when the Declaration's spirit had been deployed to justify a deep new rupture, when secession was a looming fact rather than a merely theoretical possibility—at that moment, surely it would have seemed more natural to emphasize less disruptive civic principles. Instead, Lincoln doubled down on the Declaration, insisting on its centrality to the country's identity. As historian Mark E. Neely relates, Lincoln consulted Daniel Webster's second "Reply to Hayne," a famous speech in favor of national union, when writing his first inaugural address. Webster, though, had not given pride of place to the Declaration in his argument. That was Lincoln's distinctive contribution.[33]

Kateb notes that Lincoln regarded the Declaration as one of "his holiest scriptures."[34] The other scripture for Lincoln was the Constitution, which he famously described as a frame of silver around the Declaration's apple of gold.[35] The Declaration spoke for the spirit of independence and implied a rhythm of politics, but it did not establish a means for containing and modulating that rhythm. Though not often viewed from this perspective, the Constitution has, as one of its primary purposes, the channeling of these political dynamics. Understanding the regular pattern that republics tend to fall into, anticipating and managing it, is a crucial part of the work of governing ourselves.

The Constitution aims to establish a tamed version of the political rhythm implicit in the Declaration. Instead of allowing for episodic bloody revolutions, it establishes regular ways of guiding spirited discontent into changing rulers, giving us a chance to vent our frustrations at our leaders by removing them from politics.[36] The messy, tumultuous campaigns for office, filled with accusations, recriminations, and all forms of verbal abuse, do not merely siphon off discontent; they arouse us into periods of surveillance, encouraging us to rise up in punishment of our leaders while also limiting that punishment to purely political consequences, and then they allow us to settle into longer periods of more quiescent citizenship. Though not originally a part of the constitutional plan, political parties were introduced and legitimized, by Martin Van Buren especially, to provide additional help in managing these rhythms by institutionalizing them.

Over the past few decades, with the weakening of parties and the expansion of campaigns throughout the calendar, the cadence of our politics has changed. Still, if we step back from the tumults of the moment, we can certainly sense an oscillation between periods of quiet and declarations of independence. The recent populist backlash against the growth of elite power is a part of this rhythm. To make this observation is not to diminish the danger that this populism could pose to our republican form of government if not well managed. It is merely to put the challenge into perspective. Some observers will wish we had less quiescence while others would want more stability, but the ebb and flow of political energies associated with the spirit of independence continue in a recognizable pattern. Whether these political tides will continue to be contained within the dams and dikes the Constitution and the parties have established, or whether they will burst out and swamp the whole landscape, is the question that looms over our celebration of this anniversary.

Notes

1. Niccolò Machiavelli, *Discourses on Livy*, trans. Harvey Mansfield and Nathan Tarcov (Chicago: University of Chicago Press, 1998), D 3.1, 3.17, 3.22.

2. Abraham Lincoln, "Address Before the Wisconsin State Agricultural Society" (speech, Wisconsin Agricultural Society, Milwaukee, WI, September 30, 1859), https://www.abrahamlincolnonline.org/lincoln/speeches/fair.htm.

3. Frederick Douglass, "What to the Slave Is the Fourth of July?" (speech, Corinthian Hall, Rochester, NY, July 5, 1852).

4. Stephen Skowronek, *Presidential Leadership in Political Time: Reprise and Reappraisal*, 2nd ed. (Lawrence, KS: University Press of Kansas, 2011). See also the historical patterns outlined in Samuel P. Huntington, *American Politics: The Promise of Disharmony* (Cambridge, MA: Belknap Press, 1983).

5. Edmund Burke, "Speech on Conciliation with the Colonies" (speech, Parliament, London, March 22, 1775), http://press-pubs.uchicago.edu/founders/documents/v1ch1s2.html.

6. Philip Pettit, *Republicanism: A Theory of Freedom and Government* (Oxford, UK: Oxford University Press, 1997); Quentin Skinner, *Liberty Before Liberalism* (Cambridge, UK: Cambridge University Press, 1998); and Gordon S. Wood, *The Creation of the American Republic, 1776–1787* (New York: Norton, 1993).

7. John Wise, *The Churches Quarrel Espoused* (Boston, MA: J. Allen, 1717); and John Wise, *Vindication of the Government of New-England Churches* (Boston, MA: J. Allen, 1717).

8. Burke, "Speech on Conciliation with the Colonies."

9. John M. Barry, *Roger Williams and the Creation of the American Soul: Church, State, and the Birth of Liberty* (New York: Viking, 2012), 278, 283ff, 341n13.

10. Thomas Jefferson, letter to Edward Carrington, 1787, in *American Political Thought: A Norton Anthology*, ed. Isaac Kramnick and Theodore J. Lowi (New York: W. W. Norton, 2009), 359–60.

11. Thomas Jefferson, letter to R. C. Weightman, June 24, 1826, https://www.loc.gov/resource/rbpe.15300100/?st=text.

12. "What country can preserve it's [*sic*] liberties if their rulers are not warned from time to time that their people preserve the spirit of resistance?" Thomas Jefferson, letter to William Smith, November 13, 1787, https://www.loc.gov/exhibits/jefferson/105.html. "No society can make a perpetual constitution, or even a perpetual law. The earth belongs always to the living generation." Thomas Jefferson, letter to James Madison, September 6, 1789, https://founders.archives.gov/documents/Madison/01-12-02-0248.

13. Jack N. Rakove, ed., *The Annotated U.S. Constitution and Declaration of Independence* (Cambridge, MA: Belknap Press, 2009), 22–23.

14. Kermit Roosevelt III, *The Nation That Never Was: Reconstructing America's Story* (Chicago: University of Chicago Press, 2022), 38–52.

15. Stephen A. Douglas, "Remarks of the Hon. Stephen A. Douglas, on Kansas, Utah, and the Dred Scott Decision" (speech, State House, Springfield, IL, June 12, 1857), https://www.gilderlehrman.org/collection/glc00358.

16. George Kateb, *Lincoln's Political Thought* (Cambridge, MA: Harvard University Press, 2015), 81.

17. Julian P. Boyd, ed., *The Papers of Thomas Jefferson: January 1760 to December 1776* (Princeton, NJ: Princeton University Press, 1950), 1:243–47.

18. On the Jeffersonian Republicans' use of the Declaration, see Gordon S. Wood, *Empire of Liberty: A History of the Early Republic, 1789–1815* (Oxford, UK: Oxford University Press, 2011), 641.

19. Abraham Lincoln, "Speech of Hon. Abram Lincoln, in Reply to Judge Douglas" (speech, State House, Springfield, IL, June 26, 1857), https://www.gilderlehrman.org/collection/glc02813.

20. Lincoln, "Speech of Hon. Abram Lincoln, in Reply to Judge Douglas."

21. Abraham Lincoln, letter to George Robertson, August 15, 1855, https://www.abrahamlincolnonline.org/lincoln/speeches/robert.htm.

22. Lincoln, "Speech of Hon. Abram Lincoln, in Reply to Judge Douglas."

23. Lincoln, "Speech of Hon. Abram Lincoln, in Reply to Judge Douglas."

24. John Stuart Mill, "The Contest in America," in *The Collected Works of John Stuart Mill*, ed. John M. Robson (Toronto, Canada: University of Toronto Press, 1984), 21:142.

25. Jonathan Boucher, "On Civil Liberty, Passive Obedience, and Non-Resistance," in *American Political Thought*, ed. Keith E. Whittington (New York: Oxford University Press, 2017), 115–16.

26. Boucher, "On Civil Liberty, Passive Obedience, and Non-Resistance."

27. Kenneth L. Deutsch and Joseph R. Fornieri, eds., *Lincoln's American Dream: Clashing Political Perspectives* (Washington, DC: Potomac Books, 2005), 107–8.

28. Dennis C. Rasmussen, *Fears of a Setting Sun: The Disillusionment of America's Founders* (Princeton, NJ: Princeton University Press, 2021), 12–13.

29. Boucher, "On Civil Liberty, Passive Obedience, and Non-Resistance."

30. John Locke, *Second Treatise of Government* (London: Black Swan, 1689), §§ 230, 243.

31. Machiavelli, *Discourses on Livy*, 1.5–8, 3.1.

32. Abraham Lincoln's statement of the need for a "political religion" of obedience to the laws can be found in his early speech "On the Perpetuation of Our Political Institutions," known as the "Lyceum Address."

33. Mark E. Neely Jr., *Lincoln and the Triumph of the Nation: Constitutional Conflict in the American Civil War* (Chapel Hill, NC: University of North Carolina Press, 2015), 48.

34. Kateb, *Lincoln's Political Thought*, 56, cf. 86.

35. Abraham Lincoln, "Fragment on the Constitution and Union," January 1861, https://teachingamericanhistory.org/document/fragment-on-the-constitution-and-union-2.

36. Machiavelli, *Discourses on Livy*, 1.5–8.

3

Democracy, Freedom, and the Declaration of Independence

PETER BERKOWITZ

The American Declaration of Independence and the nation it formally brought into existence in July 1776 changed the course of democracy in the West. Before the Declaration and the birth of the United States, democracy generally had a bad name. It was considered an unstable regime prone to descent into demagoguery and dictatorship. After the American founding, however, democracy came to be associated with the basic requirements of political justice. Crucial to the transformation of democracy's reputation was the distinctive alliance that the Declaration forged between democracy and the defining conviction of the modern tradition of freedom—of which the Declaration is a landmark document—that human beings are by nature free and equal.

That alliance gave birth to the regime known as liberal democracy. Today, we take the alliance for granted so much that Americans typically refer to their regime as a democracy, without modification. This simplification, however, obscures the tension between the protection of what the Declaration calls unalienable rights—the rights inherent in all human beings—and the rule of the majority. The use of the term "democracy" when liberal democracy is meant also cloaks the advantages to democracy that derive from its alliance with unalienable rights.

Over the nearly two and a half centuries, convictions about unalienable rights that gave birth to the nation but that do not belong to democracy's original and core meaning have tempered, stabilized, and elevated constitutional government in America. As the United States confronts alarming levels of discord, division, and dysfunction, it is instructive to reconsider the nation's founding principles. It is also useful to examine influential misconceptions propounded by some intellectuals about the moral and political implications of those principles and seminal lessons—ancient and modern—about democracy and freedom. A better understanding of the assumptions, ideas, and aims that spurred the transformation of 13 British colonies into the world's freest, most prosperous, and most diverse great power contributes to the restoration of that unity in diversity that remains, as it was at the founding, essential to advancing the public interest. Indeed, study of the Declaration forms a central component of liberal education, the distinctive form of civic education that is central to preserving and improving liberal democracy in the United States.

Clarifying Terms

The "liberal" in liberal democracy—which derives from the Latin *liber*, meaning free—does not refer to the political left but rather the modern tradition of freedom. That tradition antedates the contemporary distinction between left and right and has largely determined the issues over which the left and right in America have contended. The modern tradition of freedom rests on the conviction that, notwithstanding the countless differences among human beings, all are equal in basic rights. It affirms that the chief task of politics is to secure those rights. This conviction is wide and deep enough to encompass the writings of John Locke, Thomas Jefferson, James Madison, Adam Smith, Edmund Burke, Alexis de Tocqueville, John Stuart Mill, Friedrich Hayek, and Raymond Aron. It captures opinions held in common by most Americans throughout the nation's history. And of late it has been targeted by critics on both the right and the left as the principal source of the nation's ills.

Whereas the "liberal" in liberal democracy identifies a moral standard and states the major purpose of politics, the "democracy" in liberal democracy denotes the ultimate source of power in the regime. The root meaning of democracy (*demokratia*), which derives from classical Athens, is rule (*kratos*) by the people (*demos*). However, "the people" does not refer to every human being or even every individual who lives under the laws of the city or state. "The people" means the collectivity of citizens, but this neither specifies who is to be included among citizens nor prescribes to what ends or within what limits power is to be exercised.

Typically, the people equate their rule with rule of the majority. Giving expression to majority will, the people can make wise or foolish laws, and they can govern cruelly or decently. The people can establish a state religion, punish impiety, censor speech, and ostracize citizens without trial, or they can leave faith to individuals and communities, guarantee free speech, and prohibit expulsion, with or without trial. The people can provide generously through laws for the poor, the sick, the elderly, the young, and all those who cannot care for themselves; they can leave those responsibilities to citizens in their private capacities; or they can combine those approaches. The majority can rule directly by, say, gathering in the town hall or submitting all political questions to referendum on the internet. Or they can rule indirectly by delegating authority to representatives, who can be chosen by drawing lots, which reflects the egalitarian belief in equal competence, or they can be selected through elections, which rests on the aristocratic belief that citizens can and should pick the best among themselves to concentrate on governing. The people can adhere to a strict majoritarianism, according to which the preponderance of citizens has the final say, or they can restrict their discretion by entrenching various rules that limit the expression of popular will. The people can, as did classical Athens, exclude slaves, women, and anyone else they wish from political life, or they can include everybody. And, if they so desire, the people can establish a liberal democracy—that is, a democracy grounded in individual freedom and human equality that, to protect the human rights all citizens share, sets firm limits on the action a majority can take regardless of its size and the intensity of its opinion.

A liberal democracy that emphasizes the importance of the moral and civic virtues to the preservation of political liberty and the accomplishment of the common good is also called a republic, although not all republics affirm that human beings are by nature free and equal.

The Declaration's Self-Evident Truths

With the Declaration of Independence, the United States became the first nation anywhere to establish itself based on the principle "that all men are created equal, that they are endowed by their Creator with certain unalienable Rights, that among these are Life, Liberty and the pursuit of Happiness." Government's chief purpose, states the Declaration, is to secure these universal rights, which are inseparable from our humanity. To accomplish that purpose, citizens must construct a variety of political institutions. And they will need to enact and enforce a variety of positive laws and positive rights—laws and rights that are not inherent in human beings but that, when tailored to varied and changing circumstances, safeguard citizens' universal rights.

These convictions—or, as the Declaration refers to them, "self-evident" truths—stem from the convergence of several distinctive traditions. Their British heritage, stretching back to the 1215 Magna Carta and embracing the common law, the writings of John Locke, and the 1689 Bill of Rights, oriented Americans' political thinking around rights and the need to limit government power. The biblical teaching that all human beings are created in God's image (and in that sense at least are equal in relation to God) impelled Americans to provide, in a language accessible to all human beings regardless of their religious beliefs, an account of what citizens were owed by government and others in virtue of their humanity. And the civic-republican school, which derived from classical Rome and stressed the responsibilities of citizenship, connected for America's founding generation the enjoyment of freedom to the readiness of a public-spirited citizenry to defend it.

The Declaration identifies "the Laws of Nature and of Nature's God" as the source of its universal moral principles but refrains from pressing the argument. A political document intended to unite Americans and explain the justice of their break with Britain to other nations and peoples, the Declaration does not elaborate theoretical justifications in support of its grandest philosophical and theological claims. Indeed, by insisting that the truths on which the nation was founded were "self-evident," the Declaration shifts attention away from philosophy and theology to the general belief in individual freedom and human equality that was widespread among Americans.

Although it does not mention the term "democracy," the Declaration also affirms as self-evident the core democratic idea that the people rule. Governments, the Declaration asserts, acquire their "just powers from the consent of the governed." At the same time, the Declaration says nothing about the structure of government, leaving the people to determine—based on their customs, traditions, specific circumstances, and judgments—the institutional arrangements, political and civil rights, and laws best suited to securing their unalienable rights. The people needn't be directly involved in every government decision, but all exercises of government power must be traceable to their consent.

The democratic principle of rule of the people converges with the principles of modern freedom in the conviction that free and equal individuals can incur an obligation to obey a law only by consenting to it. The modern notion of consent has precursors in the biblical idea of covenant and classical ideas of political obligation. In numerous variations, modern moral, legal, and political thinkers contend that just restrictions on the freedom to choose those actions and laws best calculated to preserve oneself and promote one's happiness depend on one having chosen, in one form or another, those restrictions. Constraints on freedom are chosen well when they enhance the conditions under which freedom is enjoyed.

How effectively, though, does the theory of consent translate into practice? Does it not overlook that our habits, our beliefs about right and wrong, and our moral and political judgments derive not from considered choice alone, or even primarily, but from cultural inheritance, unwritten but widely shared norms, long-standing institutions, and common practices? What of those who lack the opportunity to consent forthrightly and explicitly to their nation's founding—that is, most people most of the time? And, whether in a self-sufficient city or in a continent-spanning nation-state, why should one who takes consent seriously obey laws that are disagreeable or downright contrary to the public interest?

The modern tradition of freedom emphasizes that consent may be not only express but also tacit. By living in a political order that secures individual rights—including the crucial right to leave—and benefiting from the laws' protection, one signals one's acceptance of laws to which one has not expressly consented. Specific laws with which one disagrees do not justify disobedience because the consent that matters for the purpose of political obligation is not to this or that law but to the constitutional framework for making, executing, and adjudicating laws. In other words, the consent that the modern tradition of freedom places at the center of political legitimacy is the agreement to comply with all the laws that emerge from the lawful operations of the constitutional process. That includes those one thinks will diminish prosperity and erode security and those that one is convinced will advance the public interest.

Consent is not a blank check. Within the boundaries of the constitutional framework, citizens are expected to oppose the laws they think disadvantageous through criticism, through peaceful protest, and, not least, through building majorities to enact better laws, implement just reforms, and renovate established institutions.

Consent, moreover, is limited by the purpose for which it is granted, which is the protection of basic rights and fundamental freedoms. Foolish government action and ill-conceived laws do not nullify consent. Impairment of rights through shortsighted legislation, clumsy or sluggish execution, or flawed judicial reasoning does not release those who live under the laws from the obligation to obey. It is only government's massive, systematic, and irreversible onslaught on citizens' unalienable rights, the protection of which is government's chief purpose, that nullifies the citizen's obligation to obey the laws.

The Declaration also regards it as self-evident that, when government destroys the conditions for securing basic rights and fundamental freedoms,

> it is the Right of the People to alter or to abolish it, and to institute new Government, laying its foundation on such principles and organizing its powers in such form, as to them shall seem most likely to effect their Safety and Happiness.

Such a right will seldom be exercised. "Prudence, indeed, will dictate that Governments long established should not be changed for light and transient causes," the Declaration stresses.

> But when a long train of abuses and usurpations, pursuing invariably the same Object evinces a design to reduce them under absolute Despotism, it is their right, it is their duty, to throw off such Government, and to provide new Guards for their future security.

Tyrannical government dissolves the grounds for consenting to state authority; therefore, revolution, in such extreme and unusual circumstances, is not a violation of the citizen's duty but an expression of it.

Three Influential Misconceptions

Some modern critics have promulgated three influential misconceptions connected to the self-evident truths affirmed by the Declaration of Independence. One, disdainful of the modern tradition of freedom, argues that universal rights and consent are a disastrous scam. A second diminishes the scope of majority decision-making in the name of democracy. A third, also in the name of democracy, enlarges and emboldens expressions of the popular will to the detriment of freedom. All three erode the balance of democracy and freedom woven into the Declaration.

Call the first misconception "the disdain-and-dismiss strategy." It comes in right-wing and left-wing versions.

According to the right-wing version, the Declaration—like the entire modern tradition of freedom—is based on a false and pernicious understanding of human nature and reason. Rights, it is asserted, are an imaginary construct; universal claims are a mirage; and consent has no stopping point. The modern understanding of freedom, it is alleged, ultimately impels human beings to seek emancipation from all limitations and to lose themselves in greedy, heedless, and debasing pursuits. The self-destructive illusions built into the Declaration's principles, conservative critics contend, blind those who live under their sway to these perennial truths about politics and society: Men and women are social beings; custom and tradition mold opinions about justice and happiness, promote the cultivation of virtue, sustain the family, and nourish community and faith; and a well-lived life requires dedication to the common good.

The left-wing version of the disdain-and-dismiss strategy agrees with the right-wing version that rights are a false and pernicious invention and universal claims are a mirage. But instead of seeing the Declaration's principles as a vehicle for the chimerical quest for total freedom, progressive critics view them as a mechanism for perpetuating racism, sexism, and sweeping inequalities of power, wealth, and status. One variant of the left-wing critique argues that unalienable rights—particularly religious liberty and economic freedom—create domains largely set off from government supervision that permit individuals to preserve and reproduce biases that underwrite systemic oppression. A more aggressive variant contends that rights and consent are themselves instruments used by dominant racial or ethnic majorities to oppress minorities.

Both the right-wing and left-wing versions of the disdain-and-dismiss strategy blame the nation's founding principles principally and often exclusively for what they most detest in America today. Both ignore, among other things, the link between the nation's founding principles and the purposes they cherish. On the one hand, conservative critics disregard the close connection between unalienable rights and consent and the limitations on government that protect families, communities, and faith. On the other hand, progressive critics overlook the force of unalienable rights and consent as a standing reproach to the injustices they denounce and as a crucial source of inspiration to reformers who have advanced the cause of equality to which progressive critics profess devotion.

The second misconception might be called "the Rousseauean gambit." Receiving its classic expression in Rousseau's account in *The Social Contract* of "the general will," the Rousseauean gambit has been enthusiastically used over the past several decades by progressive professors of political theory and law. It radicalizes the notion of tacit consent by ascribing democratic supremacy to laws and public policy that intellectuals determine to be in the people's best interest, regardless of the majority's expressed preferences and not infrequently contrary to majority wishes. These professors purport to discern through a variety of thought experiments designed to model moral and political reason—an original position, an ideal speech situation, an imagined colloquy of reasonable people—what men and women would agree about specific questions of law and policy if only they had been properly educated and their judgment had not been corrupted by upbringing and social environment, selfishness and greed, ignorance and superstition, class interests, or bigoted opinions about race, ethnicity, and sexual and gender orientation.

The Rousseauean gambit accomplishes a breathtaking inversion. In the people's name and for democracy's sake, it shifts democratic legitimacy from choices made in the voting booth by actual majorities to choices made by professors in faculty seminars, academic conferences, and scholarly writings about the decisions ordinary men and women would make if they understood their true interests. The intellectuals' insistence on preserving the term "democracy" for what amounts to rule by the highly educated and well credentialed attests to democracy's prestige. It also reveals the extent to which the intellectuals presume to have overcome their own implicit biases, narrow interests, and desire for wealth, status, and power to understand the people's interests better than do the people themselves.

The third misconception arising out of the Declaration's principles exhibits the "refounding fallacy." Energized by the supposition that if one founding is good, many foundings must be wonderful, it attributes to every generation the right and responsibility to refound the nation. It finds support in the Declaration's affirmation of the people's right and responsibility to replace tyrannical government with "new Government, laying its foundation on such principles and organizing its powers in such form, as to them shall seem most likely to effect their Safety and Happiness." But proponents of the refounding fallacy fail to take seriously the high bar—an "absolute Despotism" that destroys the conditions for exercising basic rights and fundamental freedoms—that the Declaration sets for refounding. The presumption that in every era the people must reconsider not only the nation's basic form of government but also the character of social relations and institutions conflicts with the Declaration's teaching that foundings should be rare and exceptional events.

The refounding fallacy spawns additional confusions. It blurs the Declaration's crucial distinction between the enduring constitutional framework to which consent is given—including the conviction that human beings possess inherent rights and that government's primary purpose is to secure them—and ordinary law and policymaking, the legitimacy of which rests on their having emerged from the processes prescribed by the constitutional framework. It erodes commitment to and gratitude for the nation's formal establishment in 1776 and the Constitution's drafting, ratification, and implementation between 1787 and 1789. It truncates perspective by directing attention away from the study of America's founding principles and constitutional traditions and incentivizes short-term thinking by encouraging far-reaching change based on fleeting passions and interests. And it weakens civic cohesion by insisting that the nation is perpetually in need of revolutionary transformation.

These three fallacies are not mutually exclusive: They often arise together. The refounding fallacy combines with the disdain-and-dismiss strategy and the Rousseauean gambit to conceal the decisive role the Declaration of Independence played in inspiring those who have, across the generations, undertaken pivotal reform of the nation. This fallacy devalues America's founding principles and institutions by espousing the regular creation of new ones. The Rousseauean gambit cheapens founding principles by arguing that they mandate eminently debatable and decidedly partisan policy alternatives. And the disdain-and-dismiss strategy vilifies them as the root cause of injustice and social pathology in America.

American history offers a different perspective. Time and again, eminent reformers have advanced the cause of individual freedom and equality under law by drawing on the Declaration. They did not rewrite or replace, much less revile, America's 1776 founding principles. They effectuated and vindicated them.

The clash between America's founding principles and the realities of American politics has been decided repeatedly in favor of the founding principles. Even as the institutionalization of slavery and the constitutional protection given to it betrayed the Declaration's affirmation of unalienable rights, that affirmation of rights inherent in all human beings issued a devastating indictment of slavery. The nation violated the promise of unalienable rights in many other ways: the exclusion of women from voting, the brutal treatment of Native Americans, the post–Civil War perpetuation of racial discrimination through Jim Crow, and other forms of discrimination based on race, ethnicity, and sex and gender. But each of these has been opposed and combated precisely in the name of the Declaration's principles.

Nevertheless, criticism of the nation's founding principles flies fast and furious. Many call into question the sincerity of the nation's founders. Others contend that the principles of freedom and equality served, and continue to serve, to disguise, legitimate, and perpetuate oppression. Such dark suspicions cannot be simply dismissed. Who can doubt that the founders' hearts were impure? Who can fail to recognize that in the United States—as in every democracy under the sun—high-minded principles have been invoked to cover up or rationalize cruelty and preserve a corrupt status quo?

Many founders—prominently including slave owner Thomas Jefferson, the Declaration's principal drafter—acknowledged the searing contradiction between the affirmation of unalienable rights and the horrible reality of the state-sanctioned treatment of human beings as property:

> The whole commerce between master and slave is a perpetual exercise of the most boisterous passions, the most unremitting despotism on the one part, and degrading submissions on the other. . . . I tremble for my country when I reflect that God is just, that His justice cannot sleep forever.[1]

Contemplating slavery in America, Jefferson wrote: "Nothing is more certainly written in the book of fate than that these people are to be free."[2]

Indeed, reformers throughout American history demanded freedom for those deprived of it by appealing to the unalienable rights in which the Declaration grounded American self-government. In 1848 at Seneca Falls, Elizabeth Cady Stanton adapted Jefferson's phraseology to argue in the Declaration of Sentiments that women deserve the full panoply of rights promised by the Declaration of Independence. In 1852, freed slave Frederick Douglass in "What, to the Slave, Is the Fourth of July?" and, in 1854, abolitionist William Lloyd Garrison in "No Compromise with the Evil of Slavery" invoked the Declaration to demand the end to slavery and the full emancipation of black men and women. In 1863 in his address at Gettysburg, President Abraham Lincoln called on the nation, based on the Declaration's principles, to midwife "a new birth of freedom." In 1941, echoing the Declaration's language, President Franklin Delano Roosevelt insisted in his Four Freedoms speech that in domestic affairs the United States was committed to equal human rights and in foreign affairs to the rights of nations that stem from human rights. And in 1963, from the steps of the Lincoln Memorial, Martin Luther King Jr. proclaimed in his "I Have a Dream" speech that ending racial discrimination requires a renewed dedication to the nation's founding principles inscribed in the Declaration and institutionalized by the Constitution.

Six Enduring Lessons

Liberal democracy emerges from the blending of two related principles: Human beings are by nature free and equal, and just political power derives from the consent of the governed. The rights shared equally by all authorize the people's power while setting limits on its exercise. Within those limits, the people directly—or through their designated representatives—make laws, set priorities, allocate resources, and adopt a variety of measures to promote their security, prosperity, and general welfare. Freedom and democracy, however, neither supply all the inspiration, guidance, and judgment that yield responsible self-government nor specify the beliefs, practices, and institutions that foster virtue and prepare citizens to achieve happiness.

Fortunately, the history of political philosophy is rich with lessons pertinent to the well-being of liberal democracy in America. Some of those lessons derive from classical thinkers but apply to all democracies. Some spring from modern thinkers for whom the minimally adequate form of democracy is one that protects basic rights and fundamental freedoms.

The six lessons distilled here are not the only ones relevant to grappling with the perturbations and dislocations that roil America today, nor are the thinkers from whom they are gleaned alone in providing vital insights. But these thinkers offer particularly salient lessons at this moment. Even as it confronts internal fissures and aggressive authoritarian competitors beyond its borders, liberal democracy in America has grown confused about its constitutive elements, its governing purposes, and its necessary limitations. At the same time, it has lost sight of, or taken to fulminating against, the sources that sustain it. That something similar could be said about many other liberal democracies around the world underscores the urgency of reexamining enduring lessons about free and democratic self-government.

Thucydides furnishes the first lesson: Democracy's achievements are bound up with a common inheritance that shapes citizens' character and unites the people. In *The Peloponnesian War*, the Greek historian attributes the defeat of democratic Athens by autocratic Sparta in their 27-year military conflict to the logic of geopolitics, Athenian hubris, unpredictable natural disasters, and the virtues of Spartan autocracy. Early in his account, Thucydides presents a funeral oration—an ancestral custom to honor fallen soldiers, console the bereaved, and fortify citizens for coming battles—delivered by the Athenian statesman Pericles. Emphasizing the virtues that set Athens apart, Pericles salutes but does not dwell on preceding generations' courage in preserving the city's freedom, acquiring Athens's empire, and passing it on to subsequent generations. Nor does he, despite the military context, linger on the present generation's military virtue. Rather, he elaborates the leading features of the Athenian regime and the most splendid of the citizens' nonmilitary virtues.

Favoring the many over the few, Athenian democracy regards all citizens as free and equal while respecting and awarding merit, according to Pericles. For fear of disgrace, Athenians obey the unwritten moral code, as well as the written. The city opens its doors to foreigners, and instead of the harsh discipline central to Spartan education, it relies on the good habits born of leisure. It instills the higher virtues while checking their associated vices: "We cultivate," states Pericles, "refinement without extravagance and knowledge without effeminacy." Ordinary citizens are "fair judges of public matters," while "in our enterprises we present the singular spectacle of daring and deliberation, each carried to its highest point, and both united in the same persons; although with the rest of mankind decision is the fruit of ignorance, hesitation of reflection."[3] Notwithstanding Pericles's idealized picture of Athens, intended to fortify the people's resolve at a moment of grief and uncertainty, the larger point stands: Democratic citizens' security, prosperity, and flourishing rest on qualities of mind and character rooted in a shared way of life that is not produced by but rather undergirds the people's rule.

Plato provides the second lesson: Democracy encourages vices that destroy the people's rule. In Books VIII and IX of *The Republic*, Socrates examines the decline of regimes, from the best of them, in which philosophers rule, to tyranny, the worst. Although admirable for the diversity of human types to which it is home, democracy is the second-worst kind of regime, giving birth to tyranny, according to Socrates. Democracy is marked, in his account, by the sweet freedom to do as one pleases. It treats citizens as equals regardless of their virtues, leaving each to gratify every passing desire, as if all were of the same moral worth. It empowers the multitude to act on their preference for flatterers over noble and courageous statesmen. And it upends traditional authority and erodes customary restraints. Fathers behave childishly, and sons strut proudly. Teachers fawn on students, and students mock teachers. In general, adults ingratiate themselves with the young, while the young take on grown-up airs. Rules governing relations between the sexes grow slack. Averse to authority of any sort, democratic citizens eventually shrug off the laws, both written and unwritten.

This "extreme of freedom," maintains Socrates, ineluctably produces the extreme of slavery, which is tyranny. In the name of equality, the multitude undertakes to expropriate and redistribute the property of the rich few. Because the rich do not readily acquiesce, the people rally behind the strongest and most ruthless man, one who promises to use the most effective measures—prominently including violence, imprisonment, and worse—to make the city truly equal. This, however, results in a radical form of inequality as the people's champion concludes that he must continually accumulate power to protect himself from those who resent his strength and ruthlessness. One does not have to accept every particular of Socrates's account of democracy's inevitable descent into tyranny (or the inevitability of the descent) to grasp the destabilizing vices that democracy fosters by eroding the distinction between freedom and license and encouraging the treatment of all wants, needs, and desires as equal.

Aristotle supplies the third lesson: To enjoy its benefits and contain its flaws, democracy must be combined with other just, if partial and incomplete, claims to rule to form a balanced mixed regime. In practice, as Aristotle argues in Book IV, Chapter 11 of *The Politics*, democracy amounts to rule of the largest segment of the people, who tend to be the less well-off.

Democracy, he maintains, should be merged with oligarchy, or rule of the few, who tend to be well-off. This produces a mixed regime that Aristotle calls "polity" and that he contends is the best system that is practically obtainable in most circumstances. Mixing of claims to rule, for Aristotle, is not merely a matter of expediency. Both the well-off few and the less well-off many exhibit characteristic virtues and vices. Owing to their larger accumulations of property, citizens who are well-off have a greater stake in the political community. The acquisition of wealth and the leisure that it brings, moreover, allow for the development of skills and knowledge essential to production, commerce, finance, diplomacy, and lawmaking. Meanwhile, the many who are less well-off draw on a substantially greater fund of perceptions and experience. They demonstrate in a variety of cases more reliable judgment than do the well-off few.

For both the few and the many, typical vices accompany the typical virtues. Owing to their lives of luxury, the well-off few "tend to become arrogant and base on a grand scale," developing an aversion to being ruled and knowing only how to rule like masters. The many, disposed to be "malicious and base in petty ways,"[4] cannot rule effectively because of their neediness and because they only know how to be ruled like slaves. Accordingly, Aristotle argues, the city is best off when it incorporates into the mix a substantial middle class, which is disposed to foster the virtues of the few and of the many while tempering the vices of both—in no small measure because it is likely to value stability and peace.

These first three lessons, drawn from the classical world, are particularly valuable to us now because they speak from an age that did not take the value of democracy for granted and so could perceive its flaws and limitations with more open eyes. They clearly inform the three lessons we draw from more modern observers.

Madison contributes the fourth lesson: A rights-protecting democracy must find means for counteracting democracy's characteristic ailments that are consistent with the people's sovereignty and the limits on government imposed by individual rights. In *Federalist* 10, Madison focuses on factions—groups of citizens motivated by passions or interests contrary to the rights of individuals and groups or otherwise at odds with the public interest. History and theoretical reflection alike teach that "a pure democracy"—one in which the people rule directly, unlimited by any other moral principle or political claim—produces but cannot provide a remedy for factions: "A common passion or interest will, in almost every case, be felt by a majority of the whole; a communication and concert result from the form of government itself; and there is nothing to check the inducements to sacrifice the weaker party or an obnoxious individual," Madison writes. "Hence it is that such democracies have ever been spectacles of turbulence and contention; have ever been found incompatible with personal security or the rights of property; and have in general been as short in their lives as they have been violent in their deaths."[5]

The solution is not for government to tightly regulate action or impose uniformity of opinion, because those expedients destroy the very individual freedom that liberal democracy is established to protect. Instead, the people must create political institutions that respect the principles of freedom while cooling judgment, fostering deliberation, and incentivizing compromise.

One such institution that the Constitution incorporates is representation through elected officials. Accountable to the people, these public servants will have a personal interest in advancing the public interest through their ability to "refine and enlarge" citizens' opinions. Another remedy to the dangers of majority factions in democracy is to increase their number by enlarging the size of the nation beyond the parameters of a city, parameters traditionally thought to represent democracy's natural limits. Far from undermining America's ability to enjoy the benefits of self-government, the size of the nation and the diversity of public opinion—political, religious, sectorial, and economic—would enable the American experiment in ordered liberty to establish a stable republic. The greater the number of factions, the less chance of any one of them accumulating enough power to impair the rights of individuals or imperil the public interest. Representation and extension of the size and diversity of the nation provide remedies to liberal democracy's characteristic ailments that are consistent with liberal democracy's essential principles.

Tocqueville elaborates the fifth lesson: Political freedom furnishes a vital counterweight to the vices spawned by democracy, not least because of the opportunities it provides to exercise self-government outside formal political institutions. In the introduction to *Democracy in America*, Tocqueville argues that democracy is not merely rule of the people but also a form of life defined by an "equality of conditions" that permeates both politics and society. In politics, democracy "gives a certain direction to public spirit, a certain turn to the laws, new maxims to those who govern, and particular habits to the governed." Within society, "it creates opinions, gives birth to sentiments, suggests usages, and modifies everything it does not produce."[6] While affirming democracy's justice, Tocqueville also sought to reduce its costs. The democratic spirit loosens morals; dissolves bonds of friendship, family, and citizenship; and steers attention from human greatness and transcendent goals to mundane activities and material goods. This narrowing of imagination, lowering of standards, and impoverishment of aspirations dispose individuals to obedience to a tutelary government. Such "gentle despotism" ensures—and confines the people's interests to—security and comfort.

Tocqueville found a remedy to democracy's deleterious tendencies in civil society—that wide domain between the individual and the state made possible by limited government—where much and, often, the best parts of life are lived. For example, by distinguishing church from state, the US Constitution empowers religious faith in America to restrain the impulses and the imagination to which democracy gives free rein. It allowed religious voices to speak from outside and, in some respects, above the political realm and so offer a distinct source of authority and insight. In addition, the "art of association," whereby Americans organized themselves into a multitude of groups and organizations— charitable, civic, cultural, educational, recreational, and more—enabled citizens to take responsibility for themselves and their families and communities. Through the public-spirited virtues it fostered, Americans' proclivity to associate, argued Tocqueville, staved off "individualism," a malady to which democracy disposed citizens. Individualism did not involve egoism but rather the retreat from civic duties into a small circle of friends and family. The problem was not with friends. Nor was it with the family, which, thanks largely to women—whose greater independence under democracy Tocqueville saw as beneficial and inevitable—provided the essential moral education in America. The problem was with friends and family as substitutes for civic engagement. All in all, Tocqueville teaches, liberty under law gives citizens within civil society opportunities to cultivate moral virtues and skills of citizenship that provide remedies to democracy's disadvantages.

Mill offers the sixth lesson: Democracies grounded in respect for individual freedom require a robust conservative party and a robust progressive party. In *On Liberty*, Mill connects the need for a party of the right and a party of the left to the case for free speech. Our interest in free speech, he argues, stems in the first place from our interest in the truth. In moral and political matters, there is almost always something to be said on the other side of the question. Even wrong opinions either contain a neglected but important element of truth or offer a valuable provocation, the encounter with which strengthens appreciation of the true opinion. A crucial corollary is that free and democratic political orders depend on both "a party of order or stability, and a party of progress or reform."[7]

In principle, a single, superior mind could contain the truths that are better grasped by conservatives and those best appreciated by progressives. In practice, however,

> unless opinions favourable to democracy and to aristocracy, to property and to equality, to cooperation and to competition, to luxury and to abstinence, to sociality and individuality, to liberty and discipline, and all the other standing antagonisms of practical life, are expressed with equal freedom and enforced and defended with equal talent and energy, there is no chance

of both elements obtaining their due; one scale is sure to go up, and the other down.[8]

Owing to human fallibility—not least the propensity to confuse partial truths and congenial falsehoods for the last word on hard questions—liberty of thought and discussion is essential:

> Truth, in the great practical concerns of life, is so much a question of the reconciling and combining of opposites that very few have minds sufficiently capacious and impartial to make the adjustment with an approach to correctness, and it has to be made by the rough process of a struggle between combatants fighting under hostile banners.[9]

Mill goes so far as to argue that, on the toughest and most important questions of morality and politics, society has an urgent interest in ensuring toleration of and a thorough hearing for the minority opinion.

These lessons of free and democratic self-government may not yield concrete measures to address the burning issues of the day. But they highlight crucial factors to consider in designing laws, fashioning policies, implementing government decisions exercising discretion, and adjudicating controversies in ways that are most likely to advance the public interest in a liberal democracy.

Education for Freedom and Democracy

We must revisit such lessons and grapple with the leading misconceptions about freedom and democracy because of the failures of civic education in the United States, not least its neglect of the Declaration of Independence and its inspiring legacy.

An astonishing percentage of Americans lack basic knowledge about the assumptions, operations, and achievements of American constitutional government. The higher they rise in the educational world, the more likely are students to encounter historically illiterate depictions of America as a uniquely unjust political society. Few colleges and universities make a priority of ensuring that their undergraduate students acquire an appreciation of America's founding principles and the key historical moments in the development of the American constitutional tradition. This is in part because a dwindling number of professors remain in the academy whose training and inclinations enable them to teach (and recognize the importance of) the subject.

The proper aim of civic education in a liberal democracy is to form citizens fit for free and democratic self-government. Civic education in America, therefore, is liberal education. In the United States, liberal education should give pride of place to the Declaration of Independence, which sets forth the nation's founding principles; to the Constitution, which institutionalizes the principles of freedom; and to constitutional history, which records America's achievements and setbacks in giving legal and political expression to the principles of freedom and democracy. Liberal education in the United States should prominently feature economics, jurisprudence, and diplomacy and national defense because of their centrality to the nation's security and prosperity. It should explore America's inheritance—not least biblical and classical—because these traditions have nourished and shaped liberal democracy in America. It should teach the painful facts about racism in the United States and other forms of bigotry and injustice while examining the political heroism of the men and women who drove reform by calling the nation to honor its promise to secure for all its citizens the rights human beings share. It should consider alternative forms of government and other civilizations, the better to put America's accomplishments and transgressions in perspective. And it should feature literature, history, philosophy, and theology because they refine our understanding and invigorate our imaginations by illuminating the fundamentals of human nature and the endless complexities of the human condition.

Rightly understood and responsibly undertaken, liberal education in America not only transmits vital knowledge but also cultivates toleration of diverse opinions, curiosity and independence of thought, moderation of judgment, appreciation of the variety of ways of being human and of the many opportunities to promote the public interest, and gratitude for the freedom and prosperity to which all Americans are heirs. Such an education reflects the nation's founding principles as enduringly set forth in the Declaration of Independence and sustains liberal democracy in America.

Notes

1. Thomas Jefferson, *Notes on the State of Virginia: An Annotated Edition*, ed. Robert Pierce Forbes (1785; New Haven, CT: Yale University Press, 2022), 249–50.

2. Thomas Jefferson, *The Autobiography of Thomas Jefferson, 1743–1790* (New York: Knickerbocker Press, 1914), 77.

3. *The Landmark Thucydides: A Comprehensive Guide to the Peloponnesian War*, ed. Robert B. Strassler and trans. Richard Crawley (New York: Free Press, 1998), 253–54.

4. Aristotle, *Politics*, Book IV, chapter 11 (1295b4).

5. Alexander Hamilton et al., *The Federalist: The Famous Papers on the Principles of American Government*, ed. Benjamin F. Wright (New York: MetroBooks, 2002), 133.

6. Alexis de Tocqueville, *Democracy in America*, ed. Harvey C. Mansfield and Delba Winthrop (Chicago: University of Chicago Press, 2002), 3.

7. John Stuart Mill, *On Liberty*, ed. Gertrude Himmelfarb (London: Penguin Books, 1988), 110–11.

8. Mill, *On Liberty*.

9. Mill, *On Liberty*.

4

The Adams Declaration:
A Guide for Our Times

DANIELLE ALLEN

These days, the question of whether the Declaration of Independence can be a continuing guide for our times is highly contested. For some, Thomas Jefferson's role in its creation means the text is irreparably tainted by the legitimation of enslavement. Yet this reading of the Declaration, and of its historical moment, misses much.

The Declaration offers a story of human agency that speaks as powerfully in our own times as it did to the founding generation—and to people diverse in identity and ideology. Moreover, the Declaration contributed to the crystallization of the abolitionist movement. This is because the Declaration belongs as much to John Adams as to Jefferson. It's time that we should all come to know the story of the Adams Declaration.

In this chapter, I explain how I came to see the Declaration's continuing relevance to 21st-century Americans of all backgrounds and share the journey of discovery that then ensued. A deep dive into the text's history leads to the recognition that Adams was really its prime intellectual architect and that, thanks to Adams, the document became fundamental to the project of abolitionism. Adams never owned human beings, always thought enslavement was wrong, and actively worked to end it in Massachusetts.

This is not to say that either Adams or the document was perfect. In addition to advancing a powerful vision for self-government among free and equal citizens, both Adams and the Declaration also made some philosophical errors. Turning to the Declaration's text in our own time requires embracing those elements of its argument that the drafters got right but also correcting those components where they went astray.

Night Students and the Thrill of Agency

In 1999, in Chicago, one spring afternoon, I found myself sitting at a board table in a downtown office building with lofty views beside a friendly woman named Kristina Valaitis. About a dozen of us had gathered for a meeting of the Harold Washington Literary Prize Committee. Harold Washington had been the first black mayor of Chicago. Now deceased, he had a book prize named in his honor.

I don't remember who else was there. I don't remember the deliberations. I don't remember what books we adjudicated that day. But I do remember my conversation with Valaitis. She would eventually become a good friend, but that was our first meeting. She was director of the Illinois Humanities Council; I was an assistant professor of classics at the University of Chicago.

Valaitis was trying to establish a night course in the humanities for low-income adults who had fallen out of the educational system and were ready to get back in. The purpose of the course was not vocational instruction but reflection and empowerment. The idea was that students from lower socioeconomic contexts also deserved the chance to develop their powers of reflection and analysis by engaging with a liberal arts education—that is, schooling for free people—just like students at fancy schools, such as the University of Chicago, where I taught. Valaitis was passionate about the program but having trouble finding any university to partner with her. I listened to her description of the program and volunteered immediately to help bring the University of Chicago in.

My much beloved younger cousin Michael was in prison in Southern California at the time, and I was working hard to get him an education behind bars. He had been arrested in 1995 while a junior in high school but completed his GED before his sentencing. He speedily earned every vocational degree on offer in the various facilities he found himself in. But he wanted real learning. He wanted college.

This wasn't available inside California's prisons in the 1990s, so I'd been working to find him distance learning classes and working through all the bureaucratic complexities of making that happen. Hardcover books weren't allowed in the prison, so I had to find classes that used only softcover books, and so on. The rules were endless.

When Valaitis described the students whom she sought to recruit for her program—the Odyssey Project, as it was called—I heard my cousin's story. These were the students I wanted to teach.

The Odyssey Project would have five units—history, philosophy, art history, literature, and writing. Ultimately, I would teach in all but the art history unit. And the goal of the course was ambitious. We would give the students the same caliber education as was on offer to the well-read and well-heeled students at the University of Chicago. This presented a conundrum. Many of the students signing up for the night class hadn't even finished their high school degrees. How exactly were we going to offer them an education on par with what the University of Chicago offered?

The solution to this riddle was to teach our students with short texts. We determined we would not compromise on the quality of the material we would offer them, but we would compromise on length. For no reason other than that the Declaration of Independence is short—1,337 words— I selected it to teach in the Odyssey Project. Over time, I taught it as part of history, philosophy, and writing units. The text is that serviceable.

But beyond its usefulness, something else happened. The Declaration of Independence generated an explosion of learning in my classroom. The Declaration tells the story of colonists who surveyed their circumstances, found them wanting, and set their faces in a new direction. In that story, my students saw their own stories. They, too, had found the course of events in their lives unsatisfactory and had determined to bring about a revolution in their situations. They understood immediately the Declaration's claims about human agency and the profound value in human decision-making and responsibility for shaping the direction of a community.

Our encounters with the Declaration of Independence were so riveting and empowering that I developed a deep fascination with the text. I have gone on to study and write about it for 20 years now. That journey has led me to see how central Adams was to the story of the Declaration of Independence. The time has come to tell the story of the Adams Declaration.

The Declaration as Democratic Writing

Jefferson did historians a disservice by having his tombstone inscribed with the words "Author, Declaration of Independence." In that moment, he claimed too much. Far more honest was his comment in an 1825 letter, also from near the end of his life, that the Declaration "was intended to be an expression of the American mind, and to give to that expression the proper tone and spirit called for by the occasion."[1] Or his comment in an 1823 letter to James Madison that he "did not consider it as part of my charge to invent new ideas altogether, and to offer no sentiment which had ever been expressed before."[2]

Jefferson drafted the Declaration as a member of a committee on which Adams (of Massachusetts), Benjamin Franklin (of Pennsylvania), Roger Sherman (of Connecticut), and Robert Livingston (of New York) were also members. The committee met and discussed the Declaration's arguments and structure, creating minutes to document their discussions. They agreed that Jefferson would write the first draft.

Jefferson did so quickly, in a day or two, and returned to Adams and Franklin for feedback. They provided substantive alterations. Jefferson finalized the text and sent it to the whole committee, which approved it, and then sent it to Congress, which further edited the document, deleting about 25 percent of the draft and making substantively significant additions. The drafting committee itself met before, during, and at the end of the drafting process.[3]

In other words, the Declaration was very much a product of democratic writing—many voices working together to develop something that could be endorsed despite divergences in identity and ideology.[4] Jefferson certainly played a leading role, but he was not alone in developing its intellectual architecture. On this front, Adams played the other especially important role.

Adams on Happiness

Adams of Massachusetts and Richard Henry Lee of Virginia were among the busiest members of the Continental Congress in 1775 and 1776. The two of them drove the political processes that led to the Declaration of Independence. Adams's 15-point to-do list, when he returned to the new session of Congress in February 1776, included "the Confederation to be taken up in paragraphs" (item 1), "an alliance to be formed with France and Spain" (item 2), "Government to be assumed in every colony" (item 4), and "Declaration of Independency" (item 14). All of that was well underway by July 4, 1776.[5] For Adams, the overarching goal shaping all this work was, in his vocabulary, pursuit of the happiness of the people.

Adams and Lee had been laying the groundwork for the Declaration. In the fall of 1775, the colony of New Hampshire was suffering through the absence of any functional government, because the royal governor had been driven out by radicals during the summer. They wrote to the Continental Congress seeking advice on what to do. Adams led, and Lee served on, the committee that delivered the resolution providing the advice on November 3:

> Resolved, That it be recommended to the provincial Convention of New Hampshire, to call a full and free representation of the people, and that the representatives, if they think it necessary, establish such a form of government, as, in their judgment, will best produce the happiness of the people, and most effectually secure peace and good order in the province, during the continuance of the present dispute between G[reat] Britain and the colonies.[6]

Then Adams and Lee met to discuss precisely how such new governments might be formed. They met on the evening of November 14, 1775, to begin sketching the kinds of governments that states should adopt if they succeeded in displacing the various royal administrations governing each state. In a follow-up letter to Lee, Adams sketched out his ideas for governments with three branches and separations of powers and concluded,

> In adopting a Plan, in some Respects similar to this, human Nature would appear in its proper Glory asserting its own moral Dignity, pulling down Tyrannies, at a single Exertion and erecting such new Fabricks, as it thinks best calculated to promote its Happiness.[7]

Thus, Adams introduced to the conversation the idea that happiness might govern the thinking of members of Congress about the purpose of government and linked that idea to a separation-of-powers framework. Jefferson was not using either framework in his own writings at this time.

Having laid an intellectual foundation for both independence and self-governing constitutionalism, Adams proceeded to lead Massachusetts to take the advice of Congress. Like New Hampshire, Massachusetts was without a functional royal government. Adams drove Massachusetts forward, to both declare its independence and establish a new independent government to replace the royal administration.

Massachusetts took this important step with a declaration made on January 19, 1776, which Adams drafted. Scholars have heretofore overlooked this document; even Pauline Maier in *American Scripture: Making the Declaration of Independence* had not found it. It is in its core points and language a first draft of the Declaration of Independence. Here it is, from opening to close, excerpted:

> The frailty of human Nature, the Wants of Individuals, and the numerous Dangers which surround them, through the Course

of Life, have in all Ages, and in every Country impelled them to form Societies, and establish Governments.

As the Happiness of the People *<alone>*, is the sole End of Government, So the Consent of the People is the only Foundation of it, in Reason, Morality, and the natural Fitness of things: and therefore every Act of Government, every Exercise of Sovereignty, against, or without, the Consent of the People, is Injustice, Usurpation, and Tyranny.

It is a Maxim, that in every Government, there must exist Somewhere, a Supreme, Sovereign, absolute, and uncontroulable Power: But this power resides always in the Body of the People, and it never was, or can be delegated, to one Man, or a few, the great Creator having never given to Men a right to vest others with Authority over them, unlimited either in Duration or Degree.

When Kings, Ministers, Governors, or Legislators therefore, instead of exercising the Powers intrusted *<to their Care>* with them according to the Principles, Forms and Proportions stated by the Constitution, and established by the original Compact, prostitute *<it>* those Powers to the Purposes of Oppression; to Subvert, instead of Supporting a free Constitution; to destroy, instead of preserving the lives, Liberties and Properties of the People: they are no longer to be deemed Magistrates vested with a Sacred Character; but become public Enemies, and ought to be resisted. *<by open War>*

The Administration of Great Britain, despising equally the Justice, the Humanity and Magnanimity of their Ancestors, and the Rights, Liberties and Courage of Americans have, for a Course of *<Twelve>* years, laboured to establish a Sovereignty in America, not founded in the Consent of the People, but in the mere Will of Persons a thousand Leagues from Us, whom we know not, and have endeavoured to establish this Sovereignty over us, against our Consent, in all Cases whatsoever.

The Colonies during this period, have recurr'd to every [peaceable Resource] in a free Constitution, by Petitions and Remonstrances, to [obtain justice;] which has been not only denied to them, but they have been [treated with unex]ampled Indignity and Contempt and at length open War [of the most] atrocious, cruel and Sanguinary Kind has been commenced [against them.] To this, an open manly and successfull Resistance has hith[erto been made.] Thirteen Colonies are now firmly united in the Conduct of this most just and necessary War, under the wise Councils of their Congress. . . .

. . . Mankind has seen a Phenomenon without Example in the political World, a large and populous Colony subsisting in [great] Decency and order, for more than a Year <without Government> under such a suspension of Government.

But as our Enemies have proceeded to such barbarous Extremities commencing Hostilities upon the good People of this Colony, and with unprecedented [Malice] exerting their Power to spread the Calamities of Fire, Sword and Famine through the Land, and no reasonable Prospect remains of a speedy Reconciliation with Great Britain, the Congress have resolved "That no Obedience being due to the Act of Parliament for altering the Charter of the Colony of Massachusetts Bay . . . it be recommended to the Provincial Convention to write Letters: to the Inhabitants of the several Places which are intituled to Representation in Assembly requesting them to chuse such Representatives, and that the Assembly, when chosen, do elect Councillors; and that such Assembly and Council exercise the Powers of Government. . . ."

In Pursuance of which Advice, the good People of this <*Province*> Colony have chosen a full and free Representation of themselves, who, being convened in Assembly have elected a Council, who, <*have assumed*> as the executive Branch of Government have constituted necessary officers <*civil and Military*> through the Colony. The present Generation, therefore, may be congratulated on the Acquisition of a Form of Government, more immediately in all its Branches under the Influence and Controul of the People, and therefore more free and happy than was <*ever*> enjoyed by their Ancestors. . . .

In Council January 19th. 1776

Ordered that the foregoing Proclamation be Read at the opening of Every Superior Court of Judicature &c. and Inferiour Courts of Common Pleas and Courts of General sessions for the Peace within this Colony by their Respective Clerks and at the Annual Town meetings in March in Each Town and it is hereby Recommended to the several Ministers of the Gospel throughout this Colony to Read the Same in their Respective Assemblys on the Lords Day next after their Receiving it immediately after Divine Service.[8]

With this proclamation for Massachusetts, Adams had helped model the playbook for the transition from colony to state. He hoped all the other colonies would follow. Working with Lee, he began to spread his arguments and playbook. He published a pamphlet called "Thoughts on Government: Applicable to the Present State of the American Colonies" in April 1776. Lee converted part of the pamphlet into a poster so that its circulation would be even wider.[9] The pamphlet reinforced Adams's argument that the focus of thinking about constitutional design should be on the happiness of the people and that this would be best executed through a separation of powers.

With regard to happiness, Adams wrote in the pamphlet:

> We ought to consider, what is the end of government, before we determine which is the best form. Upon this point all speculative politicians will agree, that the happiness of society is the end of government, as all Divines and moral Philosophers will agree that the happiness of the individual is the end of man. From this principle it will follow, that the form of government, which communicates ease, comfort, security, or in one word happiness to the greatest number of persons, and in the greatest degree, is the best.[10]

In invoking this idea of the happiness of society—or the ease, comfort, and security of the individuals making up society—Adams was converting into 18th-century American English an ancient Roman ideal articulated by the orator and statesman Cicero: *salus populi suprema lex esto*, or "the health and well-being of the people are the supreme law."[11] This means that any question of governmental policy should be evaluated from the perspective of whether it enables the basic human flourishing of a society and its members. The preamble to the Constitution renders the same idea with the phrase "the general Welfare."

On May 15, 1776, Adams proposed a resolution in Congress whose purpose was to begin converting the philosophical arguments about individual and social happiness into actual policy for all the colonies, just as had already been accomplished in Massachusetts. The time had come to spur the colonists into establishing governments as independent states.

To achieve this, Adams proposed that Congress vote on the following resolution:

> Resolved That it be recommended to the respective assemblies and conventions of the United Colonies, where no Government sufficient to the Exigencies of their affairs have been hitherto established, to adopt such Government as shall in the

Opinion of the Representatives of the People best conduce to the happiness and safety of their Constituents in particular and America in general.[12]

The philosophical heart of the Declaration—its second sentence—traces exactly this sort of link between the happiness of the individual and of society, identifying as the purpose of government to secure that collective safety and happiness:

We hold these truths to be self-evident, that all men are created equal, that they are endowed by their Creator with certain unalienable Rights, that among these are Life, Liberty and the pursuit of Happiness. —That to secure these rights, Governments are instituted among Men, deriving their just powers from the consent of the governed, —That whenever any Form of Government becomes destructive of these ends, it is the Right of the People to alter or to abolish it, and to institute new Government, laying its foundation on such principles and organizing its powers in such form, as to them shall seem most likely to effect their Safety and Happiness.

This was just the sort of argument that Adams had been developing throughout 1775 and 1776.

Just as Jefferson brought various materials from his work in Virginia—for instance, George Mason's Declaration of Rights—into the drafting of the Declaration of Independence, so too Adams brought his own writings and arguments. He brought the broad framework connecting the responsibilities of government to both an individual aspiration to happiness and a shared safety and happiness. He also brought in the constitutional theory used to organize the list of grievances against the king, where legislative, judicial, and executive power concerns are treated in order. Jefferson had not previously constructed his own writings around either of these intellectual frameworks.

Adams, the Declaration, and Abolition

Perhaps the most important location in the Declaration where we can see Adams's influence is in the phrase "Life, Liberty and the pursuit of Happiness."

As we have seen, Adams was the leading proponent throughout 1775 and 1776 of including the concept of "happiness" in the Declaration. The conventional formulations of 17th- and 18th-century political philosophy treated basic rights as consisting of life, liberty, and property. John Locke, for instance, argued that "being all equal and independent, no one ought to harm another in his life, health, liberty, or possessions."[13] In other words, happiness displaced property in the conventional formulation of basic rights.

At stake was the topic of enslavement. In December 1775, the royal governor of Virginia decreed that any enslaved person who fled bondage and fought for the British would be rewarded with emancipation. For some six months, he had been considering such a proclamation, and its likely occurrence had been widely rumored. When the proclamation came, the Virginians considered it an interference with their rights of property. One Virginian wrote to George Washington, who was absent from Virginia with the army, "Our Dunmore has at length Publishd his much dreaded proclamation—declareg Freedom to All Indented Servts & Slaves (the Property of Rebels) that will repair to his majestys Standard—being able to bear Arms."[14]

After Dunmore's proclamation, any active defense of the right to property was also necessarily a defense of the practice of enslavement. Adams's arguments for a picture of the basic purpose of government as turning instead around happiness must be read in that context—as providing alternative language that would avoid serving as a de facto defense of enslavement. Adams and his wife, Abigail, exchanged letters on the subject of the Virginians. She wrote to him that she thought the Virginians had "been shamefully duped by a Dunmore. I have sometimes been ready to think that the passion for Liberty cannot be Eaquelly Strong in the Breasts of those who have been accustomed to deprive their fellow Creatures of theirs."[5]

That the questions of slavery and rights of property became hopelessly entangled is clear in debates about the Articles of Confederation. Here is one telling exchange from July 30, 1776:

> *Lynch.* If it is debated, whether their Slaves are their Property, there is an End of the Confederation. Our Slaves being our Property, why should they be taxed more than the Land, Sheep, Cattle, Horses, &c.? Freemen cannot be got, to work in our Colonies. It is not in the Ability, or Inclination of freemen to do the Work that the Negroes do. Carolina has taxed their Negroes. So have other Colonies, their Lands.

> *Dr. Franklin.* Slaves rather weaken than strengthen the State, and there is therefore some difference between them and Sheep. Sheep will never make any Insurrections.

> *Rutledge.* . . . I shall be happy to get rid of the idea of Slavery. The Slaves do not signify Property. The old and young cannot work. The Property of some Colonies are to be taxed, in others not. The Eastern Colonies will become the Carriers for the Southern. They will obtain Wealth for which they will not be taxed.[16]

Adams's focus on happiness offered a form of compromise—a term open-ended enough that many could imagine their ends encapsulated by it; the phrase was also indefinite enough not to entail any kind of necessary ongoing commitment to the practice of enslavement.

That there were two frameworks for thinking about basic rights—and pressure on the question of what language would be used—is clear from the Declaration of Rights drafted by Mason for Virginia in May 1776. Mason employed both the traditional focus on property and Adams's focus on safety and happiness. Mason's declaration begins by declaring that all men are by nature equally free and independent and have certain inherent rights, of which, when they enter into a state of society, they cannot, by any compact, deprive or divest their posterity; namely, the enjoyment of life and liberty, with the means of acquiring and possessing property, and pursuing and obtaining happiness and safety.[17]

But by the time the Declaration of Independence was written, Adams had won. The concept of happiness supplanted the concept of property, a moment of compromise in the draft of the text that opened space for an abolitionist vision.

As scholar Eric Slauter has shown, the writers and pamphleteers who used the Declaration of Independence in ensuing decades were primarily abolitionists, who drew on precisely its all-important second sentence to advance the cause of emancipation and an end to slavery.[18] For instance, in Massachusetts, a free African American, Prince Hall, drew on the Declaration's language to seek abolition of enslavement in Massachusetts via a petition to the general court in January 1777.[19] He wrote: "[Negroes] have, in Common with all other men a Natural and Unalienable Right to that freedom which the [Great] Parent of the [Universe] hath bestowed equalley on all menkind." Their enslavement was a "Violation of Laws of Nature and [of] Nations."[20]

The drafters of Vermont's constitution in 1777 created the first modern government to abolish enslavement formally. They wrote in their preamble:

All men are born equally free and independent, and have certain natural, inherent, and unalienable rights, amongst which are the enjoying and defending life and liberty, acquiring, possessing, and protecting property, and pursuing and obtaining happiness and safety: therefore, no male person born in this country, or brought from over sea, ought to be holden by law, to serve any person as a servant, slave, or apprentice, after he arrives to the age of twenty one years, nor female in like manner, after she arrives to the age of eighteen years.[21]

Adams kept the work up in Massachusetts as well. He drafted the Constitution for the state of Massachusetts and drew, once more, on the language of his January 1776 Massachusetts Declaration and the July 4 national Declaration to establish a bedrock commitment to rights. As originally passed, the Massachusetts Constitution of 1780 began:

> The end of the institution, maintenance, and administration of government, is to secure the existence of the body politic, to protect it, and to furnish the individuals who compose it with the power of enjoying in safety and tranquility their natural rights, and the blessings of life; and whenever these great objects are not obtained, the people have a right to alter the government, and to take measures necessary for their safety, prosperity, and happiness. . . .

> All men are born free and equal, and have certain natural, essential, and unalienable rights; among which may be reckoned the right of enjoying and defending their lives and liberties; that of acquiring, possessing, and protecting property; in fine, that of seeking and obtaining their safety and happiness.[22]

The Massachusetts Constitution did not formally outlaw enslavement, but it did support the achievement of abolition before the end of the Revolutionary War. On the basis of the new Constitution, an enslaved woman named Elizabeth Freeman sued for her freedom in 1781. At a jury trial, Massachusetts Chief Justice William Cushing instructed a jury that enslavement had in fact been outlawed by the state's new constitution, and consequently, Freeman won her case. In 1783, the state's supreme judicial court then affirmed that constitutional interpretation.

Pennsylvania, too, passed an emancipation act before the end of the Revolutionary War, ending enslavement (albeit on an elongated timetable) in that state in 1780. This was thanks in no small measure to Franklin's work. A colleague on the Declaration drafting committee alongside Adams and Jefferson, Franklin had by the time of the Declaration's drafting come to oppose enslavement, despite having owned people earlier in his life.

In sum, Adams's work from 1775 to 1783 forged a linked agenda of independence, self-government, and abolition. This would eventually become the American agenda. It was and is a profoundly democratic agenda.

The "Masculine System" and Its Limits

Of course, Adams's voice was not the only one shaping the Declaration of Independence. While he succeeded at forging compromises that ultimately helped crystallize abolitionism, other moments in the Declaration entrenched enslavement. The text the committee submitted to Congress included language condemning King George for a trade that violated "the sacred rights of life and liberty" of people in distant Africa. The draft, in other words, equally acknowledged European-descended colonists and Africans as holding the same sacred rights. Congress, however, excised this language from the draft.[23] From the perspective of the enslavement-practicing South, it went too far.

The first founding philosophy for our country was far from entirely perfect in all its details, nor was Adams a perfect democrat. But Adams and other founders clearly did genuinely believe that all human beings have basic natural rights. Their beliefs were sufficiently robust to achieve the abolition of enslavement in three former English colonies (Massachusetts, Pennsylvania, and Vermont) by 1783.

Nonetheless, they did not allocate power throughout society in accordance with this view. To the contrary, they reserved power largely to white male property holders, and they increased the degree of that restrictiveness over time. While property-holding women, for instance, had voting rights in some states after the revolution, in the wake of the Constitution, those rights were eroded. In 1807, New Jersey was the last state to remove voting rights from women.[24]

Adams and his contemporaries were not oblivious to the disjunction between the broad claims about universal human rights and structures of power that allocated the right of political participation only to some. Two people who wrote to Adams to raise questions about this were fellow Bostonian James Sullivan and Adams's own wife, Abigail.

On May 9 and 17, 1776, Sullivan, a politician, wrote to Adams to advocate for assigning voting rights to men without property in the newly forming polity.[25] On May 26, Adams responded to reject the argument:

> Your Idea, that those Laws, which affect the Lives and personal Liberty of all, or which inflict corporal Punishment, affect those, who are not qualified to vote, as well as those who are, is just. . . .

> [But] the Same Reasoning, which will induce you to admit all Men, who have no Property, to vote, with those who have, for those Laws, which affect the Person will prove that you ought to admit Women and Children: for generally Speaking, Women and Children, have as good Judgment, and as independent Minds as those Men who are wholly destitute of Property: these last being to all Intents and Purposes as much dependent upon others, who will please to feed, cloath, and employ them, as Women are upon their Husbands, or Children on their Parents.[26]

Abigail similarly wrote to raise questions about the rights of women. That spring, in March 1776, Abigail wrote to John to inquire about the progress of the revolution and women's place in it. She was eager to see independence. She also urged him to "remember the ladies." She wrote:

Remember the Ladies, and be more generous and favourable to them than your ancestors. Do not put such unlimited power into the hands of the Husbands. Remember all Men would be tyrants if they could. . . .

That your Sex are Naturally Tyrannical is a Truth so thoroughly established as to admit of no dispute, but such of you as wish to be happy willingly give up the harsh title of Master for the more tender and endearing one of Friend. Why then, not put it out of the power of the vicious and the Lawless to use us with cruelty and indignity with impunity.[27]

She warned him that if the new government did not do more to incorporate women's interests, "we are determined to foment a Rebellion, and will not hold ourselves bound by any Laws in which we have no voice, or Representation."[28] John's response to Abigail was to insist that male power could be wielded beneficently. "Depend upon it," he wrote,

We know better than to repeal our Masculine systems. Altho they are in full Force, you know they are little more than Theory. We dare not exert our Power in its full Latitude. We are obliged to go fair, and softly.[29]

Annette Gordon-Reed and Peter Onuf have offered a close and compelling analysis of how Jefferson developed a paternalistic theory of government—rights might pertain to all humanity, but it was the job of some to protect others and secure their safety and happiness.[30] Adams, too, subscribed to this paternalistic theory of authority.

In doing so, Adams and his colleagues depended on one important clause in the Declaration to bring a seeming coherence out of the incoherence that all might have rights even when some governed—and even owned—others. That clause, once again, appears in the all-important second sentence. Let's take one more look at it, focusing closely this time on the final clause.

We hold these truths to be self-evident, that all men are created equal, that they are endowed by their Creator with certain
unalienable Rights, that among these are Life, Liberty and the
pursuit of Happiness, —That to secure these rights, Governments are instituted among Men, deriving their just powers
from the consent of the governed, —That whenever any Form
of Government becomes destructive of these ends, it is the
Right of the People to alter or to abolish it, and to institute new
Government, *laying its foundation on such principles and organizing its powers in such form, as to them shall seem most likely to effect
their Safety and Happiness.* (Emphasis added.)

The final distinction between the foundation of principle on which
the new government was grounded and the procedures for organizing
the powers of the government permitted and sustained the paternalistic
approach. Adams's answers to both Sullivan and his wife were, in essence,
that, yes, the concepts of rights, personal liberties, and aspirations to
well-being pertained to everyone, but when it came to how the powers
of government would be organized, those powers would be reserved for
some—namely, white male holders of property ("our masculine systems")
to wield on behalf of all. The idea of separability between the basic principles and the allocation of power sustained the founding's contradictions.

On May 7, in response to Adams's April 12 reply that he and his colleagues were unlikely to adopt Abigail's approach to a code of laws, she
chastised him:

I can not say that I think you very generous to the Ladies,
for whilst you are proclaiming peace and good will to Men,
Emancipating all Nations, you insist upon retaining an absolute power over Wives. But you must remember that Arbitrary
power is like most other things which are very hard, very lia-
ble to be broken—and notwithstanding all your wise Laws and
Maxims we have it in our power not only to free ourselves but

to subdue our Masters, and without violence throw both your
natural and legal authority at our feet.[31]

Abigail named the key philosophical error of the founding generation—
to think that one could achieve the protection of rights for all while
reserving power only to some. As she wrote, unlimited power tempts
people into tyrannical behavior. We might say that absolute power cor-
rupts absolutely. Abigail thus identified the most important philosophical correction that would have to be made in the ideas of the founding
generation for a firm foundation for democracy to be secured. To protect
the rights of all, all must share in power. The work required is to lay the
foundations of a political system on a set of principles that protect basic
rights but also organize the powers of government in such a form that all
can share in those powers, thereby ensuring that the safety and happiness
of the people will be secured.

Realizing the democratic potential of the Declaration of Independence
requires completing the long-fought-for transition from the paternalistic
liberalism of the 18th century to power-sharing liberalism, the cause of
our times.

A Guide for Our Times

Histories of American political thought and politics have oscillated
between the idea that the founding ideals were essentially complete
and required only an unfolding realization in practice and the idea
that the founding ideals are irrecoverably marred by various forms of
domination—of people of African descent, women, and Indigenous people. These two positions lead to two different approaches for how we
should currently make use of our founding era's texts. Those in the former camp believe the texts as they stand can serve as an unproblematic
guide for us, as we work to ascertain at the level of concrete policy and
organizational structure how better to realize them. Those in the latter

camp argue instead that we should throw out these documents and start over, perhaps even have a new constitutional convention and draft from scratch.

I offer a third perspective. If we take the time to figure out precisely where the founders were conceptually right and where they went conceptually wrong, we can build on the good and take on the responsibility of correcting the bad. Achieving self-government for free and equal citizens under a condition of full inclusion isn't simply a matter of changing laws and policies to better match the stated ideals of the founding. We actually have to do some work to improve the ideas of the founding too.

After we do that philosophical work, we have to develop laws and policies that align with those improved ideals. The specific conceptual improvement needed is the one named by Abigail Adams—the recognition that building a society based on the rights of all, for the sake of the safety and happiness of all, requires that power be shared by all. With that important conceptual improvement clearly in view, we can take on founding work in our own era and for our generations, seeking as our ancestors did to understand how best to secure a free society in contemporary conditions.[32]

Notes

1. Thomas Jefferson, letter to Henry Lee, May 8, 1825, in *The Writings of Thomas Jefferson*, ed. Paul Leicester Ford (New York: Knickerbocker Press, 1899), 10:343, quoted in Pauline Maier, *American Scripture: Making the Declaration of Independence* (New York: Knopf Doubleday Publishing Group, 1997).

2. Thomas Jefferson, letter to James Madison, August 30, 1823, in *The Writings of Thomas Jefferson*, ed. Paul Leicester Ford (New York: Knickerbocker Press, 1899), 10:268, quoted in Maier, *American Scripture*.

3. Maier, *American Scripture*, 101–2.

4. Danielle Allen, *Our Declaration: A Reading of the Declaration of Independence in Defense of Equality* (New York: Liveright, 2014), 47.

5. Allen, *Our Declaration*, 59; and John Adams, diary, 25:6–7, [February?] 1776, Adams Family Papers, Massachusetts Historical Society.

6. Worthington Chauncey Ford, ed., *Journals of the Continental Congress, 1774–1789* (Washington, DC: Government Printing Office, 1904–37), 3:319.

7. Allen, *Our Declaration*, 58–60; and John Adams, "From John Adams to Richard Henry Lee, 15 November 1775," Founders Online, https://founders.archives.gov/documents/Adams/06-03-02-0163.

8. The text in brackets was deleted. Founders Online, "IV. A Proclamation by the General Court, 19 January 1776," https://founders.archives.gov/documents/Adams/06-03-02-0195-0005.

9. Allen, *Our Declaration*, 59.

10. Founders Online, "III. Thoughts on Government, April 1776," https://founders.archives.gov/documents/Adams/06-04-02-0026-0004.

11. Cicero, *On Laws*, 3.3.8.

12. John Adams, "[Wednesday May 15. 1776]," Founders Online, https://founders.archives.gov/documents/Adams/01-03-02-0016-0120.

13. John Locke, *Second Treatise of Government* (1690; Indianapolis, IN: Hackett Publishing Company, 1980), chap. 2.6, https://www.gutenberg.org/files/7370/7370-h/7370-h.htm.

14. Lund Washington, "To George Washington from Lund Washington, 3 December 1775," Founders Online, https://founders.archives.gov/documents/Washington/03-02-02-0434.

15. Abigail Adams, "Abigail Adams to John Adams, 31 March 1776," Founders Online, https://founders.archives.gov/documents/Adams/04-01-02-0241.

16. John Adams, "[Notes of Debates on the Articles of Confederation, Continued] July 30. 1776.," Founders Online, https://founders.archives.gov/documents/Adams/01-02-02-0006-0008-0003.

17. Virginia Declaration of Rights, § 1.

18. Eric Slauter, "The Declaration of Independence and the New Nation," in *The Cambridge Companion to Thomas Jefferson*, ed. Frank Shuffelton (Cambridge, UK: Cambridge University Press, 2009), 27–28.

19. Danielle Allen, "A Forgotten Black Founding Father," *The Atlantic*, February 10, 2021, https://www.theatlantic.com/magazine/archive/2021/03/prince-hall-forgotten-founder/617791.

20. Massachusetts Historical Society, "Petition for Freedom to the Massachusetts Council and the House of Representatives, January 13, 1777," https://www.masshist.org/database/557.

21. Vt. Const. ch. I, art. I.

22. Mass. Const. pmbl.; and Mass. Const. pt. I, art. I.

23. Allen, *Our Declaration*, 137.

24. Museum of the American Revolution, "When Women Lost the Vote: A Revolutionary Story, 1776–1807," https://www.amrevmuseum.org/virtualexhibits/when-women-lost-the-vote-a-revolutionary-story.

25. James Sullivan, "To John Adams from James Sullivan, 9 May 1776," Founders Online, https://founders.archives.gov/documents/Adams/06-04-02-0075.

26. John Adams, "From John Adams to James Sullivan, 26 May 1776," Founders Online, https://founders.archives.gov/documents/Adams/06-04-02-0091.

27. Adams, "Abigail Adams to John Adams, 31 March 1776."

28. Adams, "Abigail Adams to John Adams, 31 March 1776."

29. John Adams, "John Adams to Abigail Adams, 14 April 1776," Founders Online, https://founders.archives.gov/documents/Adams/04-01-02-0248.

30. Annette Gordon-Reed and Peter S. Onuf, *"Most Blessed of the Patriarchs": Thomas Jefferson and the Empire of the Imagination* (New York: Liveright, 2016).

31. Abigail Adams, "Abigail Adams to John Adams, 7 May 1776," Founders Online, https://founders.archives.gov/documents/Adams/04-01-02-0259.

32. Portions of this chapter draw on Allen, *Our Declaration*.

5

Lincoln's Declaration and
the Coherence of Democracy

GREG WEINER

Abraham Lincoln's "Fragment on the Constitution and the Union"[1] famously compares the relation between the Declaration of Independence and the Constitution to Proverbs 25:11's reference to "apples of gold in pictures of silver." His point is that the mechanisms of the Constitution (the picture) serve the ideals of the Declaration (the apple). This is often understood to indicate Lincoln's emphasis on individual rights as the lens through which the Constitution should be interpreted. Yet the timing of the fragment, presumed to have been written between his election as president in 1860 and his inauguration in 1861, suggests otherwise. He wrote the fragment at the same time he was drafting his first inaugural address, a full-throated defense of democracy understood as majority rule.[2]

In that speech, he declared: "A majority, held in restraint by constitutional checks, and limitations, and always changing easily, with deliberate changes of popular opinions and sentiments, is the only true sovereign of a free people." The nation divided naturally into majorities and minorities on questions over which the Constitution gave the national government jurisdiction. "If the minority will not acquiesce," Lincoln explained, "the majority must, or the government must cease. There is no other alternative; for continuing the government, is acquiescence on one side or the other."[3]

That is also what the Declaration says when read in full. Yet scholarship on Lincoln's view of the Declaration, the Constitution, individual rights, and the relationship among the three substantially rotates around the assumption of some degree of tension. That is the enduring debate, though contemporarily recast, between Harry Jaffa and his intellectual descendants and those who saw Lincoln's theory of personal rights as a "derailment" of the American tradition. (With the acerbity for which he was famed, Jaffa was wont to associate these thinkers with John C. Calhoun and describe them with epithets like "neo-Confederate.")[4]

Might the very terms of this debate, inescapably inflected with 20th-century controversies, including the Civil Rights Movement and the rise of the Warren Court's activism in the name of individual rights, miss the Declaration's point—and, with it, Lincoln's? Put otherwise: Lincoln might find the terms of the debate over his legacy unintelligible in his own dialect. Lincoln's position can be articulated simply and, it should be said, entirely in keeping with the teachings of the Constitution's framers. Participation in democratic self-rule is both a right and the only viable political means of securing, as opposed to simply proclaiming, other rights. Individual rights and the common good are not opposing notions, and neither are individual desires and communal aims. A democratic republic exists to pursue them together.

By considering the terms of this debate, we might not only shed light on Lincoln's understanding of the Declaration of Independence but also better grasp the character of American democracy and the legacy of our founding.

The House Divided

Jaffa's breakthrough and now canonical study of the Lincoln-Douglas debates, *Crisis of the House Divided*, understands the two statesmen's essential division over the limits of majority rule. Stephen Douglas was morally indifferent to enslavement and thus happy to leave the issue to "popular sovereignty." But Lincoln thought individuals' most fundamental liberty was not subject to majority rule. The converse also held. Jaffa wrote in the introduction to the 50th-anniversary edition of *Crisis*:

Lincoln, however, insisted that the case for popular government depended upon a standard of right and wrong independent of mere opinion and one which was not justified merely
by the counting of heads. Hence the Lincolnian case for government of the people and by the people always implied that
being for the people meant being for a moral purpose that
informs the people's being.[5]

Jaffa's claim is that Lincoln, like Socrates in Plato's *Republic*, denies that
justice is the rule of the stronger.

Yet two issues are latent in this claim, and a full understanding of Lincoln hinges on separating them. One is what is just—which Lincoln certainly did not associate with "the counting of heads." The other is the
mechanism for attaining justice, which, as Lincoln understood, unavoid-
ably involved counting heads. His refutation of Douglas's doctrine of popular sovereignty indicates as much. Lincoln's famous characterization of
this notion of popular sovereignty distilled it to the claim "that if any *one*
man, choose to enslave *another*, no *third* man shall be allowed to object."[6]
(Emphasis in original.) Jaffa, noting that Lincoln "picked his words
with utmost precision," understands the warning to be the universaliz-
ing nature of Douglas's claim: There could be no principle that justifies
enslaving black Americans that did not at the same time justify enslaving
white Americans—or anyone else.[7]

As will be shortly seen, Jaffa's claims that Lincoln was a statesman,
an axiomatic thinker, and a meticulously precise writer are not entirely
compatible. Axioms are clean and precise; politics is messy and opaque.
More important, Jaffa's analysis glosses over crucial elements of Lincoln's case. Lincoln's horror at the Kansas-Nebraska Act, which enshrined
Douglas's doctrine of popular sovereignty, was *not* that it subjected
individual freedom to plebiscites. Lincoln surely wished for a virtuous
political order in which no such plebiscite was necessary. But the question at stake was at what level of government the decisions should be
made.

Lincoln stated this principle clearly in his 1854 Peoria address. The immediate problem was not the legality of enslavement per se but that the Missouri Compromise had already settled the question at the national level—because permitting more states to enslave people had national repercussions. This was the import of the "house divided" address:

> In my opinion, [the slavery controversy] will not cease, until a crisis shall have been reached, and passed. . . . Either the opponents of slavery, will arrest the further spread of it, and place it where the public mind shall rest in the belief that it is in course of ultimate extinction; or its advocates will push it forward, till it shall become alike lawful in all the States.[8]

In other words, the national government had the authority to regulate enslavement because it was inescapably a national issue.

None of this detracts from Lincoln's horror at the evil of slavery. He ardently wished its "ultimate extinction" and always had. But we must read him as a statesman and not as a professor. In that sense, the popular-sovereignty issue is better understood as a question of federalism: At its core, was this a local or a national issue? Lincoln was no Garrisonian; he did not reject the Missouri Compromise, which permitted enslavement in some states. He objected to empowering individual states to make that decision without regard to its national implications.

We can see this more clearly by looking more closely at Lincoln's simple summary of popular sovereignty: If one individual enslaves a second individual, no third individual can object. If Lincoln's reading of the Declaration was focused on personal rights, what business is it of the third individual to be involved at all? One man's attempt to enslave another is prima facie unjust. There is no need, and indeed there is every injustice, in allowing a third person to participate in deciding the question—whether he objects or not. Lincoln's question is *who* the third man is. It is the national and not the local electorate.

The purpose of the foregoing is not to shear Lincoln of his profound and genuine moral orientation to politics by reducing his analysis of popular sovereignty to legal formalisms. But for a country lawyer who thought in axioms—a manner of thought Jaffa admires—forms matter. Adherence to forms provided the means for moral consensus.

Jaffa's dismissal of neo-Confederates, whom he viewed as intellectual descendants of Calhoun, rests in part on the claim that their reading of the Declaration, unlike Lincoln's, focused on corporate rather than individual rights. This, again, was inextricable from Jaffa's inability to resist the ad hominem argument. Adherents of this view were largely (though not exclusively) Southerners at a time when the justice of the Confederate cause was widely considered an open question. Two things may be true. One is that certain Southerners among this group were guilty of, if not neo-Confederate sympathies, at least romanticizing the intellectual depth of the secessionists who precipitated the Civil War. The second is that their reading of the Declaration might still require serious engagement.

In *The Basic Symbols of the American Political Tradition*,[9] Willmoore Kendall and George W. Carey (from Oklahoma and Illinois, respectively) assessed the American regime through the lens of the "new science of politics" proposed by Eric Voegelin.[10] They traced the character and development of polities in terms of the symbols through which they understood their engagement with reality. When those symbols went awry, the polity's understanding of reality changed, a moment that later Voegelinians labeled "derailment."[11]

Through a careful assessment of American political development beginning with the Mayflower Compact, Kendall and Carey concluded that the "basic symbol" of America is "self-government by a virtuous people." That implies, among other things, legislative supremacy leavened by deliberation, a consistent foundation of early American institutions. Kendall and Carey asked whether the Declaration represents a derailment. Their answer was that it does not. The Declaration speaks of the acts of "one people," not isolated individuals; it creates new sovereignties but self-consciously avoids proclaiming a new nation; and the bill of particulars against King George III consists mostly of offenses against either "virtue" (for example, he has "destroyed the lives of our people") or self-government ("suspending our legislatures," among other acts).

On the other hand, Kendall and Carey concluded, *Lincoln's* Declaration, both as he described it and as his later admirers extended his argument, *did* trigger a derailment. They charged Lincoln, especially at Gettysburg, with several mistakes. One is setting the nation's beginning in 1776 rather than, for example, at the Mayflower Compact or any number of other moments that symbolized deliberative self-government. Moreover, Lincoln seems to ascribe constitutional status to the Declaration. Most important, he elevates equality as the supreme symbol of the American tradition—ignoring the other "self-evident" truths Jefferson proclaimed, including the Declaration's reference to "the consent of the governed" being the only foundation of "just powers." Subsequent egalitarians, Kendall and Carey regretted, have extended this symbol of equality from a repudiation of enslavement all the way to a guarantee of equal social, economic, and political outcomes.

Latter-day egalitarians and individualists see the Constitution in progressive terms, as an undemocratic, even antidemocratic document and a departure from the Declaration's ideals—as evidenced by the founding generation almost immediately realizing their error and adding the Bill of Rights. In this view, the Declaration, like humanity after the fall from Eden, descends into aristocracy before beginning a recovery under Lincoln and reaching its apotheosis in progressivism. Kendall and Carey argued that this understanding misreads both the Bill of Rights—whose "father," James Madison, described it largely in terms of rights regulable by the mechanisms of self-government—and history. Bills of rights were common devices in the pre-constitutional period, and the debate about a similar instrument at the national level well preceded Madison's proposal of one after the Constitution went into effect.

Rights and Self-Government

Here we arrive at a point at which these two camps—Jaffa and his individualist students on the one hand and Kendall, Carey, and their fellow advocates of deliberative self-government on the other—may speak past one another on a crucial point on which Lincoln himself shows no signs of confusion.

One bit of evidence Jaffa offered—perhaps the only credible bit of evidence—for the accusation of neo-Confederate sympathies among his opponents was that those opponents shared with Calhoun a corporate understanding of the Declaration of Independence. Calhoun did articulate such an understanding, and he did so often. He insisted the Declaration meant to argue that it was the states as corporate bodies, not the individuals living in them, that were equal to each other. Consequently, no other state had the authority to impose policies, whether tariffs or restrictions on enslavement, on South Carolina without South Carolina's consent.[12]

But this is not the argument Kendall and Carey make about self-government. Their understanding follows from a deeper problem in the Declaration—its claim that the rights to "life, liberty, and the pursuit of happiness" are "inalienable." In law, to alienate something is to give it away in exchange for an equivalent—for example, a person selling a house alienates it in exchange for the purchase price. Understood in this way, the Declaration's self-evident rights are obviously alienable if we understand them to apply to individuals.

We can push the point further. The alienation of limitless natural rights in exchange for regulable civil rights is the entire basis of social-contract theory. From Thomas Hobbes to John Locke to Jean-Jacques Rousseau and beyond, the individual gives up their pre-political right to act without boundaries in exchange for civil rights that are limitable. Civil rights constitute an equivalent because natural rights cannot be meaningfully enforced outside a political context. In the American understanding, as in the British before it, the best guarantor for rights is deliberative self-government in which everyone equally participates. What an entire people cannot do is alienate its right to self-government to another people, which was in effect what the British Empire asked the colonists to do. On *this* corporate understanding of rights, a people's corporate right to self-government includes the populace's responsibility to protect individual rights while adjusting them to political life and the common good.

To develop this understanding fully, we must return briefly to Locke, the theorist widely presumed, with good reason, to be the most significant influence on the Declaration. The vast bulk of Locke's *Second Treatise of Government* pertains to the purposes for and methods by which governments are formed.[13] A reader who stops at the formation of government will misunderstand Locke as much as a reader who relishes the opening poetry in the Declaration of Independence but skips the actual grievances.

Individualist readers of Locke ignore, as do individualist readers of the Declaration, the difference between natural and civil rights—that the state of nature's independent rights do not, and in fact cannot, transfer to a civil state. That would defeat the purpose of a society banding together in the first place. In paragraph 95 of the *Second Treatise*, Locke explains that human beings are naturally free and independent—words that appear in the Declaration's first draft. Crucially, though, freedom and independence are exercised *in*, not *after*, the act of forming society. He writes: "When any number of men have so consented to make one community or government, they are thereby presently incorporated, and make one body politic, wherein the majority have a right to act and conclude the rest."[14]

And why must the body politic be bound by the majority? Locke answers in paragraph 96. Because a political community is "one body" and "must move one way," he explains,

> it is necessary the body should move that way whither the greater force carries it, which is the consent of the majority, or else it is impossible it should act or continue one body, one community, which the consent of every individual that united into it agreed that it should.[15]

Compare that phrase—the commonwealth *must* move and majority rule is the only way it can—with Lincoln's understanding that, in the absence of majority rule, society would cease. Locke's invocation of "force" is also suggestive. It echoes both Madison's and Lincoln's understanding that republican societies cannot do what is right and just without the majority's support, so moral ideals are attainable only with moral suasion. That is an inherent moral hazard for the statesman. He is inevitably open to accusations of injustice because building the consensus that makes it possible to do right takes time.

Locke's readers may reasonably wonder why they had to slog through 94 paragraphs that hint at individual rights only to throw it all away in paragraph 95. One explanation—quite compatible with the Declaration's explanation and Lincoln's—is that Locke's account of society's purposes is a common reference for persuading the apparently all-powerful majority to behave rationally. We might think of it this way: If a group of students pooled money to form a book-buying collaborative and later a majority of them decided to spend the funds on a night out, stopping them might be difficult. But the others could at least appeal to the original purposes of their compact. Madison made exactly this argument in introducing the Bill of Rights. He was aware, he said, that "paper barriers" could not impede determined majorities. But

> as they have a tendency to impress some degree of respect for them, to establish the public opinion in their favor, and rouse the attention of the whole community, it might be one means to control the majority from those acts to which they might be otherwise inclined.[16]

In briefer form, the Declaration follows precisely Locke's structure—rhetorical grounding followed by the mechanisms by which a just society makes decisions. The Declaration's rhetorical preamble states several self-evident truths. One is that all men are equally entitled to life, liberty, and the pursuit of happiness. So far, so good, at least for the Lockean individualist account. But the next truth is "that to secure these rights, Governments are instituted among men, deriving their just powers from the consent of the governed." That is the moment of exercising freedom and independence—the transition from natural to civil rights. The third self-evident truth, the right to revolution, refers to a return to the state of nature in which the protections of civil laws can no longer be invoked— what Locke famously calls an "appeal to heaven."[17]

The actual grievances that follow can be counted and categorized differently. But the single largest category—roughly 12 of the grievances— pertains to King George inhibiting republican self-government. The king has dissolved legislatures, convened them at distant places, refused to approve good laws, and so forth. Even many of the allegations that pertain to rights are based on the regulation of liberty by republican processes, such as imposing taxes "without our consent" and maintaining standing armies "without the Consent of our legislatures."

Ultimately, the entire Declaration is a persuasive brief—which suggests that the revolutionary generation did not believe, with Thomas Paine, that people could change their form of government for any reason and on any occasion.

Lincoln's Declaration

What, then, did Lincoln's Declaration mean? To read him with an innocent eye, unaware of interpretive controversies, is to see that pitting the Declaration's equality and attendant personal rights against the Constitution's devotion to republican self-government is not simply a false dichotomy; it is a dichotomy stated in a language Lincoln does not speak.

Lincoln's patois was equality, and both the Declaration and the Constitution derived from that principle. He never betrayed any indication that he felt he was contradicting himself. Lincoln described the Declaration as the fount of every political opinion he had ever had;[18] it was the "electric cord" binding generations of Americans.[19] Yet his "beau ideal of a statesman" was Henry Clay, who was devoted to compromise on the issue of enslavement to preserve the Constitution and Union.[20] When Lincoln told his longtime friend Joshua Speed that most Northerners "crucify their feelings [about enslavement], in order to maintain their loyalty to the constitution and the Union," he rued the tension but did not deny its necessity.[21]

In some ways, Jaffa's reading of Lincoln as more scholar than statesman is defensible, even if that reading exists in tension with itself. Lincoln thought the principles of the Declaration rose from "definitions and axioms"; he often cited Euclid in their defense.[22] But he was also a prudent statesman who understood that stating ideals and attaining them were compatible things but still different. Indeed, Lincoln explained as early as 1858, and most extensively at Cooper Union, that the founders knew the Declaration's ideals would take time:

> They grasped not only the whole race of man then living, but they reached forward and seized upon the farthest posterity. They erected a beacon to guide their children and their children's children, and the countless myriads who should inhabit the earth in other ages.[23]

En route to Washington for his 1861 inauguration, Lincoln frequently invoked the Declaration. He wanted to save the Union and the principle of equality. "But, if this country cannot be saved without giving up that principle—I was about to say I would rather be assassinated on this spot than to surrender it," he said at Independence Hall in Philadelphia.[24] Significantly, Lincoln did not say he *would* sacrifice one to the other. Still less did he believe it would be necessary. The anguish was directed at himself; he would rather be assassinated than have to make the exchange. Moral suasion within constitutional boundaries was the only way to avoid it.

Lincoln's commitment to self-government is latent in the terms in which he condemned the doctrine of popular sovereignty. The essential question was where sovereignty properly resided. But he also mocked Douglas for leaving the issue of enslavement to popular sovereignty while professing moral agnosticism. Douglas was, as Lincoln once lampooned him, the only man in America who had no opinion on slavery. Apologists for slavery were actually zealots for it, Lincoln said in Peoria. What he most hated was not the concept of voting on rights but rather doing so unmoored from moral commitments. The essential claim of popular sovereignty was that "there is no right principle of action but *self-interest*."[25] (Emphasis in original.) Lincoln thought there were higher principles. The Declaration contained them. But both it and the Constitution provided mechanisms for their attainment.

The Republican Principle

How can one hold these commitments to Euclidean principle and statesmanlike prudence—which require the accommodation of principle to circumstance—at the same time?[26] To do so seems fraught with problems. Suppose Lincoln could have abolished slavery by sidestepping republican processes. He had opportunities. In August 1861, for example, Maj. Gen. John C. Frémont issued an order declaring martial law in Missouri and emancipating people enslaved by Confederates. Lincoln reversed the order, citing prudential concerns—such as alienating the border state of Kentucky—but also constitutional ones. He enclosed a recent act of Congress governing such actions and told Frémont to conform to it.[27]

Some readers, citing Lincoln's wartime censorship, suspension of habeas corpus, and similar measures, have understood him to have deliberately violated the Constitution. Noah Feldman, for example, argues that Lincoln deliberately fractured the "compromise Constitution" to elevate it to "the moral Constitution."[28] Yet Lincoln saw compromise as a moral act unto itself, one rooted in humility and devotion to the common good. A centerpiece of his opposition to the Kansas-Nebraska Act had been that it repealed the Missouri Compromise *as* a compromise. Lincoln worked assiduously to keep the most intense controversies, including the controversy over the Fugitive Slave Act, out of the Republican convention in 1860. He pacified the border states that permitted slavery because he knew the Union would be lost if they left it.

Lincoln's moderation and gradualism on the issue of slavery, which he believed were necessary to reconcile the principle of equality as expressed in both liberty and consent, exposed him to abuse. Even in the White House, he tinkered with schemes of gradual emancipation that would have taken the institution of slavery into the dawn of the 20th century. In an interesting passage from an 1859 speech in Chicago, Lincoln addressed these difficulties:

> The Republican principle, the profound central truth that slavery is wrong and ought to be dealt with as a wrong, though we are always to remember the fact of its actual existence amongst us and faithfully observe all the constitutional guarantees—the unalterable principle never for a moment to be lost sight of that it is a wrong and ought to be dealt with as such. . . .

> I suppose [slavery] may long exist, and perhaps the best way for it to come to an end peaceably is for it to exist for a length of time. But I say that the spread and strengthening and perpetuation of it is an entirely different proposition.[29]

Is there not something deeply immoral in this toleration of slavery—as there was, equally arguably, in his first inaugural speech's pledge to abide by the Constitution's fugitive-slave clause, a particular and perhaps unrivaled cruelty that required the return of those who had tasted freedom to their prior chains? By reversing Frémont, Lincoln surely consigned people to enslavement, just as he did by limiting the Emancipation Proclamation to enslaved people in Confederate states but not those loyal to the Union. If the Declaration and Constitution were in tension with one another—if the former was the apple and the latter the picture—should Lincoln not have done all he could, as quickly as he could, however he could, to emancipate enslaved people?

Of course, the statesman has no choice but to hazard the purity of his conscience. He cannot always indulge his immediate moral urges, no matter how right they may be, because doing so can imperil their long-term security.

But a deeper answer rests at the heart of Lincoln's simultaneous devotion to the Declaration and Constitution. To see it, we must pay adequate attention to Lincoln's equation, in the passage from the 1859 Chicago speech above, of the "Republican principle" with the wrongness of slavery. We have seen that republicanism was a *means* of ending slavery and achieving the ideals of the Declaration. But this claim is different. It is that the principle is actually the same. The idea of equality dictated *both* that everyone could participate in self-government *and* that no one could enslave other people.

In fact, Lincoln said at one of his 1858 debates with Douglas, the Declaration's devotion to equality was most clearly expressed in democratic terms. The Declaration's whole series of self-evident truths culminated in the fact that governments derived just powers *"from the consent of the governed,"* Lincoln explained. (Emphasis in original.) "If that is not Popular Sovereignty, then I have no conception of the meaning of words."[30]

This is the foundation for the argument he makes for majority rule in his first inaugural speech. The Southern states, not the electoral majority, were repudiating the principle of constitutional republicanism. He professed fidelity to the Constitution, including its protections for slavery. He promised to interpret the document according to its plain meaning, not "hypercritical rules." The whole of the speech is a prudent accommodation of his principles to the rules of the Constitution. On the eve of the 1864 presidential election, which Lincoln could have lost—in which case the Union would have been lost—he defended the people's right to end the Civil War through democratic processes. "It is their own business," he said, "and they must do as they please with their own."[31]

We must return here to the underlying moral dilemma stated above. How could a man who possessed power and saw the right in Euclidean terms endorse—not merely tolerate—its subjection to democratic processes? Why should anyone have to convince a majority of his or her basic rights or even, in the case of enslavement, his or her humanity? In the messy context of political life, as Lincoln knew, there simply is no other way—as much as we might wish it were not so—that rights can actually be secured. The Declaration said as much in stating the self-evident truth that governments were instituted to secure rights. If their just powers then arise from consent, citizens have no choice but to persuade one another. If we are to achieve democratic ideals, including the equality that is the basis of democracy itself, persuasion might even be a moral duty. Without it, we cannot assume the virtue on which self-government depends, nor can we simultaneously enjoy equality in the mutual senses of freedom and consent.

In that sense, the debate over Lincoln (or the Declaration or Locke) is miscast as purely one between majority rule and individual rights. It is, rather, a choice between personal independence on the one hand and a truly common good—attained by the equal right to determine it—on the other. That does not mean slavery is wrong only if the majority says so. Nor does it mean individuals must sacrifice their most essential form of human independence—freedom from slavery—to common goals.

On this question, the searing heat and moral crucible of enslavement can distort our understanding. Ordinary politics entails adjusting personal desires to common aims. Lincoln's genius, like the Declaration's, was the reconciliation of individual rights and the common good, not the choice between them. At the end of the "Fragment on the Constitution and the Union," which casts the Declaration as the apple of gold contained in the Constitution's picture of silver, Lincoln exhorts us to "act, that neither picture, or apple shall ever be blurred, or bruised or broken."[32] The "neither" indicates he saw no contradiction in preserving both. Nor need we.

Notes

1. Abraham Lincoln, "Fragments on the Constitution and the Union," Collected Works of Abraham Lincoln, January 1861, https://quod.lib.umich.edu/l/lincoln/lincoln4/ 1:264.

2. For an excellent and penetrating analysis of Abraham Lincoln's commitment to majority rule, see James H. Read, *Sovereign of a Free People: Abraham Lincoln, Majority Rule, and Slavery* (Lawrence, KS: University Press of Kansas, 2023).

3. Abraham Lincoln, "First Inaugural Address," Collected Works of Abraham Lincoln, March 4, 1861, https://quod.lib.umich.edu/l/lincoln/lincoln4/1:389.

4. See Daniel McCarthy, "Willmoore Kendall: Forgotten Founder of Conservatism," Imaginative Conservative, March 29, 2017, https://theimaginativeconservative. org/2017/03/willmoore-kendall-conservative-movement-daniel-mccarthy.html; and Glenn Ellmers, *The Soul of Politics: Harry V. Jaffa and the Fight for America* (New York: Encounter Books, 2021).

5. Harry V. Jaffa, *Crisis of the House Divided: An Interpretation of the Issues in the Lincoln-Douglas Debates* (Chicago: University of Chicago Press, 2009), xi.

6. Abraham Lincoln, "'A House Divided': Speech at Springfield, Illinois," Collected Works of Abraham Lincoln, June 16, 1858, https://quod.lib.umich.edu/l/lincoln/ lincoln2/1:508.

7. Jaffa, *Crisis of the House Divided*, 281.

8. Lincoln, "'A House Divided.'"

9. Willmoore Kendall and George W. Carey, *The Basic Symbols of the American Political Tradition* (Washington, DC: Catholic University of America Press, 1995).

10. Eric Voegelin, *The New Science of Politics: An Introduction* (Chicago: University of Chicago Press, 1987).

11. Eric Voegelin, *The Collected Works of Eric Voegelin: Anamnesis*, ed. David Walsh, trans. M. J. Hanak (Columbia, MO: University of Missouri Press, 2002), 6:384.

12. See, among other writings, John C. Calhoun, "A Discourse on the Constitution and the Government of the United States," in *Union and Liberty: The Political Philosophy of John C. Calhoun*, ed. Ross M. Lence (Indianapolis, IN: Liberty Fund, 1992), 132.

13. John Locke, *Second Treatise of Government* (Indianapolis, IN: Hackett Publishing Company, 1980).

14. Locke, *Second Treatise of Government*, para. 95.

15. Locke, *Second Treatise of Government*, para. 96.

16. James Madison, "Speech Introducing Proposed Constitutional Amendments," in *The American Republic: Primary Sources*, ed. Bruce Frohnen (Indianapolis, IN: Liberty Fund, 2002).

17. Locke, *Second Treatise of Government*, para. 20.

18. Abraham Lincoln, "Speech in Independence Hall, Philadelphia, Pennsylvania," Collected Works of Abraham Lincoln, February 22, 1861, https://quod.lib.umich.edu/l/ lincoln/lincoln4/1:376.

19. Abraham Lincoln, "Speech at Chicago, Illinois," July 10, 1858, Collected Works of Abraham Lincoln, https://quod.lib.umich.edu/l/lincoln/lincoln2/1:526.

20. Abraham Lincoln, "First Debate with Stephen A. Douglas at Ottawa, Illinois," Collected Works of Abraham Lincoln, August 21, 1858, https://quod.lib.umich.edu/l/lincoln/lincoln3/1:1.

21. Abraham Lincoln, "To Joshua Speed," Collected Works of Abraham Lincoln, August 24, 1855, https://quod.lib.umich.edu/l/lincoln/lincoln2/320.

22. Abraham Lincoln, "To Henry L. Pierce and Others," Collected Works of Abraham Lincoln, April 6, 1859, https://quod.lib.umich.edu/l/lincoln/lincoln3/1:98.

23. Abraham Lincoln, "Speech at Lewistown, Illinois," Collected Works of Abraham Lincoln, August 17, 1858, https://quod.lib.umich.edu/l/lincoln/lincoln2/1:567.

24. Abraham Lincoln, "Speech at Philadelphia," Collected Works of Abraham Lincoln, February 1, 1861, https://quod.lib.umich.edu/l/lincoln/lincoln3/1:90.

25. Abraham Lincoln, "Speech at Peoria, Illinois," Collected Works of Abraham Lincoln, October 16, 1854, https://quod.lib.umich.edu/l/lincoln/lincoln2/1:282.

26. On Lincoln's commitment to prudence, see Greg Weiner, *Old Whigs: Burke, Lincoln, and the Politics of Prudence* (New York: Encounter Books, 2019).

27. Abraham Lincoln, "To John C. Fremont," Collected Works of Abraham Lincoln, September 2, 1861, https://quod.lib.umich.edu/l/lincoln/lincoln4/1:929. John C. Frémont replied in moralistic terms, requesting that Lincoln make his order countermanding Frémont's explicit. Lincoln did so on September 8, 1861, again citing the illegality of Frémont's proclamation.

28. Noah Feldman, *The Broken Constitution: Lincoln, Slavery and the Refounding of America* (New York: Farrar, Straus and Giroux, 2021). For a defense of Lincoln's spirit of compromise, see Greg Weiner, "Lincoln and the Moral Dimension of Compromise," *American Political Thought* 11, no. 2 (Spring 2022): 253–63, https://www.journals.uchicago.edu/doi/10.1086/719356.

29. Abraham Lincoln, "Speech at Chicago, Illinois," Collected Works of Abraham Lincoln, March 1, 1859, https://quod.lib.umich.edu/l/lincoln/lincoln3/1:90.

30. Abraham Lincoln, "Speech at Edwardsville, Illinois," Collected Works of Abraham Lincoln, September 11, 1858, https://quod.lib.umich.edu/l/lincoln/lincoln3/1:13.

31. Abraham Lincoln, "Response to a Serenade," Collected Works of Abraham Lincoln, October 19, 1864, https://quod.lib.umich.edu/l/lincoln/lincoln8/1:128.

32. Lincoln, "Fragments on the Constitution and the Union."

About the Authors

Danielle Allen is a professor of public policy, politics, and ethics at Harvard University; director of the Allen Lab for Democracy Renovation at the Harvard Kennedy School of Government; and author of *Our Declaration: A Reading of the Declaration of Independence in Defense of Equality* (2014).

Peter Berkowitz is the Tad and Dianne Taube Senior Fellow at the Hoover Institution at Stanford University. He has served as director of the State Department's Policy Planning Staff, executive secretary of the department's Commission on Unalienable Rights, and senior adviser to the secretary of state.

Bryan Garsten is a professor of political science and humanities at Yale University and the author of *Saving Persuasion: A Defense of Rhetoric and Judgment* (2009).

Greg Weiner is the president of Assumption University and author of *Old Whigs: Burke, Lincoln and the Politics of Prudence* (2019).

Gordon S. Wood is professor emeritus of history at Brown University.

About the Editors

Yuval Levin is the director of Social, Cultural, and Constitutional Studies at the American Enterprise Institute, where he also holds the Beth and Ravenel Curry Chair in Public Policy. The founder and editor of *National Affairs*, he is also a senior editor at the *New Atlantis*, a contributing editor at *National Review*, and a contributing opinion writer at *New York Times*.

Adam J. White is a senior fellow at the American Enterprise Institute, where he focuses on the Supreme Court and the administrative state. Concurrently, he codirects the Antonin Scalia Law School's C. Boyden Gray Center for the Study of the Administrative State.

John Yoo is a nonresident senior fellow at the American Enterprise Institute; the Emanuel S. Heller Professor of Law at the University of California, Berkeley; and a visiting fellow at the Hoover Institution.

RESEARCH STAFF

SAMUEL J. ABRAMS
Nonresident Senior Fellow

BETH AKERS
Senior Fellow

J. JOEL ALICEA
Nonresident Fellow

JOSEPH ANTOS
Senior Fellow Emeritus

LEON ARON
Senior Fellow

KIRSTEN AXELSEN
Nonresident Fellow

JOHN BAILEY
Nonresident Senior Fellow

KYLE BALZER
Jeane Kirkpatrick Fellow

CLAUDE BARFIELD
Senior Fellow

MICHAEL BARONE
Senior Fellow Emeritus

MICHAEL BECKLEY
Nonresident Senior Fellow

ERIC J. BELASCO
Nonresident Senior Fellow

ANDREW G. BIGGS
Senior Fellow

MASON M. BISHOP
Nonresident Fellow

DAN BLUMENTHAL
Senior Fellow

KARLYN BOWMAN
*Distinguished Senior
Fellow Emeritus*

HAL BRANDS
Senior Fellow

ALEX BRILL
Senior Fellow

ARTHUR C. BROOKS
President Emeritus

RICHARD BURKHAUSER
Nonresident Senior Fellow

CLAY CALVERT
Nonresident Senior Fellow

JAMES C. CAPRETTA
Senior Fellow; Milton Friedman Chair

TIMOTHY P. CARNEY
Senior Fellow

AMITABH CHANDRA
Nonresident Fellow

LYNNE V. CHENEY
Distinguished Senior Fellow

JAMES W. COLEMAN
Nonresident Senior Fellow

ZACK COOPER
Senior Fellow

KEVIN CORINTH
*Senior Fellow; Deputy Director, Center
on Opportunity and Social Mobility*

JAY COST
*Gerald R. Ford Nonresident
Senior Fellow*

DANIEL A. COX
*Senior Fellow; Director, Survey
Center on American Life*

SADANAND DHUME
Senior Fellow

GISELLE DONNELLY
Senior Fellow

ROSS DOUTHAT
Nonresident Fellow

COLIN DUECK
Nonresident Senior Fellow

MACKENZIE EAGLEN
Senior Fellow

NICHOLAS EBERSTADT
*Henry Wendt Chair in
Political Economy*

MAX EDEN
Senior Fellow

JEFFREY EISENACH
Nonresident Senior Fellow

ANDREW FERGUSON
Nonresident Fellow

JESÚS FERNÁNDEZ-
VILLAVERDE
John H. Makin Visiting Scholar

JOHN G. FERRARI
Nonresident Senior Fellow

JOHN C. FORTIER
Senior Fellow

AARON FRIEDBERG
Nonresident Senior Fellow

JOSEPH B. FULLER
Nonresident Senior Fellow

SCOTT GANZ
Research Fellow

R. RICHARD GEDDES
Nonresident Senior Fellow

ROBERT P. GEORGE
Nonresident Senior Fellow

EDWARD L. GLAESER
Nonresident Senior Fellow

JOSEPH W. GLAUBER
Nonresident Senior Fellow

JONAH GOLDBERG
*Senior Fellow; Asness Chair
in Applied Liberty*

JACK LANDMAN GOLDSMITH
Nonresident Senior Fellow

BARRY K. GOODWIN
Nonresident Senior Fellow

SCOTT GOTTLIEB, MD
Senior Fellow

PHIL GRAMM
Nonresident Senior Fellow

WILLIAM C. GREENWALT
Nonresident Senior Fellow

JIM HARPER
Nonresident Senior Fellow

TODD HARRISON
Senior Fellow

WILLIAM HAUN
Nonresident Fellow

FREDERICK M. HESS
*Senior Fellow; Director,
Education Policy Studies*

CAROLE HOOVEN
Nonresident Senior Fellow

BRONWYN HOWELL
Nonresident Senior Fellow

R. GLENN HUBBARD
Nonresident Senior Fellow

HOWARD HUSOCK
Senior Fellow

DAVID HYMAN
Nonresident Senior Fellow

BENEDIC N. IPPOLITO
Senior Fellow

MARK JAMISON
Nonresident Senior Fellow

FREDERICK W. KAGAN
*Senior Fellow; Director,
Critical Threats Project*

STEVEN B. KAMIN
Senior Fellow

LEON R. KASS, MD
Senior Fellow Emeritus

JOSHUA T. KATZ
Senior Fellow

L. LYNNE KIESLING
Nonresident Senior Fellow

KLON KITCHEN
Nonresident Senior Fellow

KEVIN R. KOSAR
Senior Fellow

ROBERT KULICK
Visiting Fellow

PAUL H. KUPIEC
Senior Fellow

www.ingramcontent.com/pod-product-compliance
Lightning Source LLC
Jackson TN
JSHW081331130125
77033JS00014B/500

* 9 7 8 0 8 4 4 7 5 0 6 1 3 *